Praise for Mary Kole

"*Writing Interiority* is for all writers ready to level up. Once again, Mary Kole has delivered an entire master class within one volume. I was fortunate enough to work under Mary's tutelage a couple of years ago in the Story Mastermind writing program (aka the best thing I ever did for my craft), and this book is a close second. It digs into the ins and outs of developing your character's inner monologue—something many writers struggle with. Mary touches upon the concept within *Writing Irresistible Kidlit*, and this book picks up where that left off. I highly recommend *Writing Interiority* for your next craft book." - *Zane Re-Bloom*

"*Writing Interiority* is crafted for guaranteed learning. Awesome reference tool to assist your writing endeavors. The craft and techniques contained within the lines are a goldmine for those wishing to find joy and new directions in their writing. The book is written to spark maximum reading and retention so writers can unlock their full potential, understand and demystify important concepts. Mary Kole is amazing in writing talent and full mastery … only someone with understanding can make this look so simple. A very rewarding read, so stick with it, give it time—to supercharge your writing." - *Janis Smith*

"The craft world needed this book! Such a difficult concept to do right if it doesn't come naturally. This book will give me better tools to improve my skills. It was broken up so clearly and logically." - *Whitney*

"The advice is wonderful, thoughtful, and so clearly written that no writer could read *Writing Irresistible Kidlit* and not walk away with something gained from it." - *Ashlee W.*

"Writing Irresistible Kidlit is hands-down the best writing book I've read in years. It's a masterclass in a book." - *Alison S.*

"I can't begin to say how helpful *Writing Irresistible Kidlit* has been for my own writing journey." - *Joel A.*

"Writing Irresistible Picture Books is insightful, invaluable, and incredibly thorough! It's a must-have for anyone who aspires to write picture books and a great resource for those who are looking to hone their craft. I've already sent the link to writers I know." - *Elle*

"After writing a novel, unpublished writers inhabit an unguided middle space between not being important enough to warrant industry attention, and needing professional feedback to see how they stack up in the market. That is where Mary Kole lives. Her advice is sound, she pulls no punches, and if you listen to her, your work will improve." - *Andres Faza*

"Mary is a top professional in the industry and her advice is on-point and actionable. Having Mary on your team will no doubt improve your pitch, manuscript, query, or whatever you're writing." - *Elana I.*

"From now on, if I see a writing craft book with Mary Kole's name on it, I will hit the 'one click purchase' button without a second thought. She respects writers. She feels for writers. She understands writers. She knows exactly what insights writers need as they work. *Writing Irresistible Kidlit* is possibly the very best book on writing craft I have read in twenty-five years." - *Sprocket*

"Mary truly is amazing! Thanks to her, I have learned so much about writing. She made me laugh. She made me cry. She made me a better writer!" - *M. Churchill*

"Writing Interiority explains step-by-step how to create and convey character thoughts, feelings, reactions and interpretations, expectations, and inner struggles on the page. With examples from more than fifty books, it is a masterclass on the topic and I'm sure I will reference it for years to come. I've recommended it to all my writing friends as a must-read book on the topic of creating engaging characters that readers are compelled to read about. Thank you Mary for writing such an invaluable resource." - *Jamie Willis*

"I've read many books on the craft of writing, and *Writing Irresistible Kidlit* is among the best. I've never been so excited to get to the keyboard." - *Alan Harell*

"*Writing Irresistible Kidlit* is quite simply, the best 'how to' book on novel writing that I've ever read and probably ever will read in my life." - *Carol*

"Mary Kole helped me to find my way. Her suggestions on my query letter are just what I needed to begin fearlessly searching for a place to call my own. I now consider Mary Kole my secret weapon." - *Tracy*

"Mary Kole brings years of solid experience and insight to the art of writing literature for younger audiences." - *Robin*

"*Writing Irresistible Kidlit* is the perfect blend of technical 'how to' guidance mixed with a healthy dose of encouragement. If anything I write in the future ever sells, I feel I may owe Ms. Kole a royalty for her shaping input from this book." - *A. Gable*

"I'm a big fan of everything Mary Kole does and this book was no exception. I learned so much reading Mary's feedback on the various components of each query letter in *Successful Query Letters*." - *Jamie L.*

"Kole is clearly passionate about her work and the world of kidlit, and that passion spills over the pages of *Writing Irresistible Kidlit*." - *Ashley B.*

"I would highly recommend learning from Mary Kole to anyone seriously looking to improve their writing." - *Kate K.*

"Receiving Mary's feedback on my novel has been one of the best things that has happened to my writing in recent years. Thanks to her, I see the possibilities in my book and also feel like a fire has been lit under me to continue. I know the work is not yet done, but today—*today*—I feel like it's possible."
- *Anonymous*

Writing Interiority Workbook:
Your Step-by-Step Guide to Crafting Irresistible Memoir and Fiction Characters

by Mary Kole

GOOD
STORY
PUBLISHING

"Writing Interiority Workbook: Your Step-by-Step Guide to Crafting Irresistible Memoir and Fiction Characters"
By Mary Kole

1. Reference / Writing, Research, and Publishing Guides / Writing

FIRST EDITION
Print ISBN: 978-1-939162-17-5

Cover Design: Jenna Van Rooy
Cupcake Image (page 245): Jenna Van Rooy
Author Photo: Joe Ferrucci
Layout and Formatting: Kaylee Pereyra

Printed in the United States of America

This workbook has been created to stand alone,
but it's also a robust companion to:

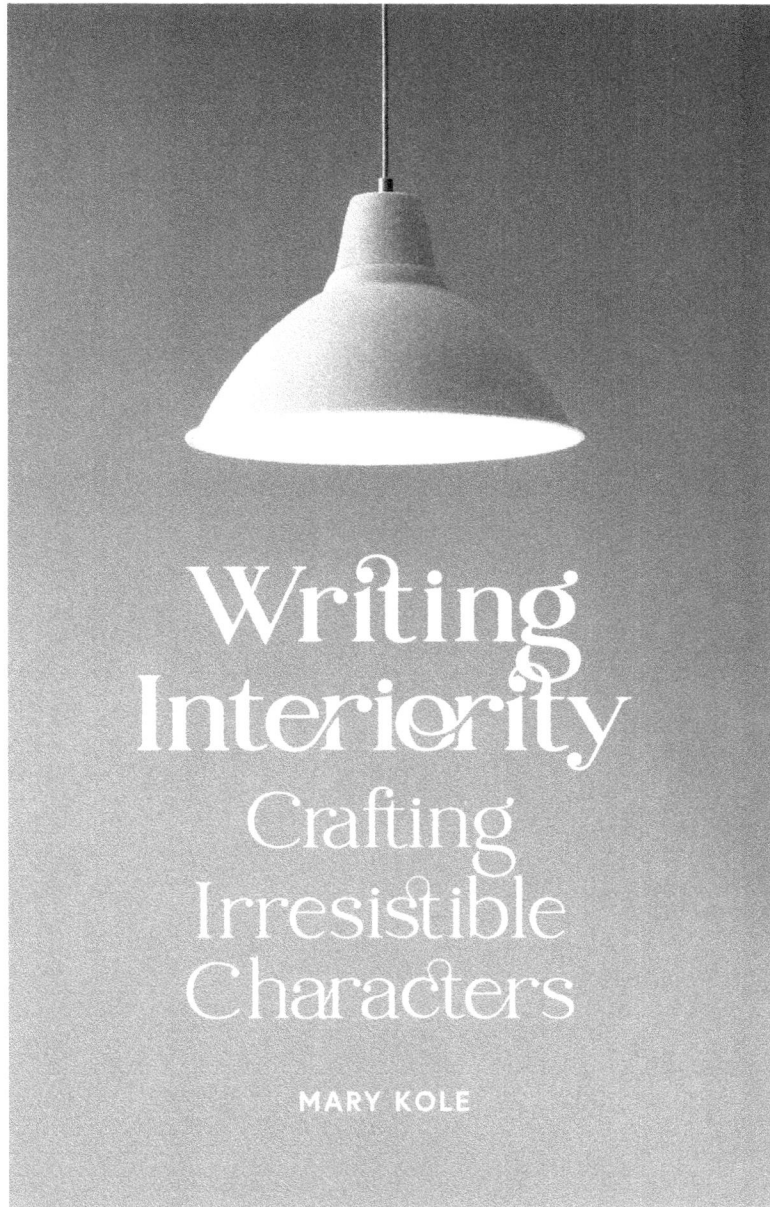

Writing Interiority
Crafting Irresistible Characters

MARY KOLE

For Todd: I've dedicated so many books to our kids,
I figured this is long overdue. I'm proud of you and I love you!

About Mary Kole

A former literary agent, Mary Kole knows the ins and outs of the publishing industry. She founded Mary Kole Editorial in 2013 to provide consulting and developmental editing services to writers across all categories and genres. She started Good Story Company in 2019 to create valuable content like the Good Story Podcast, Good Story YouTube channel, and the Writing Craft Workshop membership community. Her Story Mastermind small group workshop intensives help writers level up their craft, she offers done-for-you revision and ghostwriting with Manuscript Studio, and marketing services with Good Story Marketing.

She also develops unique and commercial intellectual property for middle grade, young adult, and adult readers with Upswell Media and Bittersweet Books, the latter with literary agent John Cusick and #1 *New York Times* best-selling author, Julie Murphy.

Mary has appeared at regional, national, and international writing conferences for the SCBWI, Writer's Digest, Penn Writers, Writer's League of Texas, San Francisco Writers Conference, WIFYR, Writing Day, and many others. Her guest lectures have taken her to Harvard, the Ringling College of Art and Design, the Highlights Foundation, the Loft Literary Center, and more. Mary's recorded video classes can be found online at Writing Mastery Academy, Writing Blueprints, Udemy, and LinkedIn Learning.

Mary holds an MFA in Creative Writing and began her publishing career with a literary agency internship and the Kidlit blog, which she started in 2009. She has worked at Chronicle Books, the Andrea Brown Literary Agency, and Movable Type Management. Her books are *Writing Irresistible Kidlit: The Ultimate Guide to Crafting Fiction for Young Adult and Middle Grade Readers*, from Writer's Digest Books/Penguin Random House, and *Irresistible Query Letters*, *Writing Irresistible Picture Books*, *Writing Irresistible Picture Books Workbook*, *How to Write a Book Now*, *Writing Interiority*, and the *Writing Interiority Workbook* from Good Story Publishing.

Originally from the San Francisco Bay Area, she lives with her three children, husband, two pugs, and a cat, in Minneapolis, MN.

Text Examples and Content Warning

This writing workbook features various original writing samples inspired by a wide variety of published works and summarizes contextually relevant elements of their plots. They are featured for the purposes of providing context and engaging you in writing exercises. Due to licensing and permissions costs, original texts are only featured in the U.S. and Canadian version of *Writing Interiority: Crafting Irresistible Characters.*

More consequentially, these stories deal with a number of potentially difficult topics, as novels and memoirs often reflect and even amplify the most dramatic events life has to offer. These topics include gender inequality, sex and sexuality, domestic and familial violence, infidelity, murder, sexual assault, child loss, immigration and deportation, mental health crisis, suicidal ideation, and self-harm. Go easy on yourself as you read if you find any of these subjects triggering, and make sure you have support. This is a writing workbook, and I would hate for the subject matter in certain excerpts to overshadow their intended educational purpose.

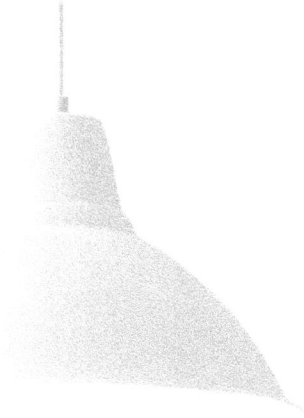

Table of Contents

Introduction   1

Part 1: Interiority Basics   3

What is Interiority?   5

Your Job as a Writer   23

Premise and Theme   39

Point of View and Plot   47

Part 2: Deep Character Development   61

Backstory and Wound   63

Sense of Self   77

Objective and Motivation   97

Need   113

Inner Struggle   131

Worldview   147

Character Arc   159

Part 3: Supporting Storytelling Elements   177

Secondary Characters   179

Information Reveals   195

Reactions and Decisions   201

Leveraging Stakes   211

Story World   219

Voice and Writing Style   229

Troubleshooting Interiority   241

Conclusion   249

Resources

Introduction

When you develop a deep understanding of your characters, you get to the root of the creative writing craft itself. Characterization is a means of discovering voice and deepening your storytelling, and the tool of interiority is essential to crafting a compelling protagonist.

Learning and practicing this concept will help you make your individual mark on the industry, whether you want to publish traditionally or try your hand at self-publishing. In this workbook, we'll add to your writing toolbox together and explore what interiority can do for you.

This book is written in three parts:
- Interiority Basics
- Deep Character Development
- Supporting Storytelling Elements

In Part 1, I'll start with a detailed presentation of the craft concept of interiority, defined as the deep exploration of a character's thoughts, feelings, reactions, expectations, and inner struggles. It's important to remember that interiority is a gray-area tool, with no set parameters or, until now, clear definition. When used effectively, it takes a manuscript to the next level. I'll discuss how to convey these elements on the page and define your most important job as a writer in today's crowded marketplace —making readers care. I'll also unpack why "show, don't tell," an important maxim in storytelling, has been responsible for leading many well-meaning creators astray. We'll also discuss premise, theme, POV, tense, and plot.

Writers often wonder how much character development they should do. In Part 2, we'll discuss all of the complex ingredients that create a layered protagonist, starting with backstory, wound, and misbelief. After you develop your character's formative experiences, you can dig into their sense of self, motivation and objective (which starts to weave in the plot), need, and internal conflict. We'll discuss worldview and how it's established, whether it changes, and how it affects reader engagement. And, finally, we'll study character arc and growth.

Part 3 is our bridge to the larger ecosystem of the story. No matter how specific a protagonist is, they need to be surrounded by context and put into motion. You'll want to populate your world with other similarly interesting secondary characters and antagonists (if applicable). As your protagonist interfaces with the story, they'll face information reveals, reactions, turning points, decisions, and stakes. Interiority allows you to juice maximum impact from the plot you've created. I'll also discuss the context of a story's world and how world-building can be used to enhance and deepen character development. Finally, we'll touch upon voice and writing style, and offer some troubleshooting tips and answers to commonly asked questions.

By harnessing the power of interiority and caring more deeply about your protagonist, you will create irresistible characters for the passionate readers who are waiting for *your* work. This is the book I've wanted to write for over a decade. I'm so thrilled to finally take you on this journey. Read on, and here's to a good story!

PART ONE

INTERIORITY BASICS

What Is Interiority?

Interiority is a brilliant creative writing concept because it's the most effective way to develop your protagonist. It's universal and useful across all writing styles, target audiences, and genres. I'll offer a top-line definition here. Don't worry if this doesn't click perfectly yet. It will.

> **Interiority:** The on-the-page rendering of your character's thoughts, feelings, reactions, expectations, and inner struggles, whether conscious or subconscious, either anchored in present time or outside of it. Interiority reveals all manner of character insights, including ideas tied to theme, premise, backstory, objective and motivation, need, worldview and morality, perspectives on other people, character relationships, reactions to plot events and information, decisions, stakes, and the story world. Interiority is also inherently tied to voice and writing style.

Though my specific terminology and conceptualization might be new, interiority is a familiar concept. Writers have been exploring this area of the craft for as long as pen has been put to paper. This workbook codifies interiority into five pillars, which encompass a character's:

- Thoughts
- Feelings
- Reactions
- Expectations
- Inner Struggles

Interiority can, honestly, be anything. A reaction to what's happening; a joke or bit of character uniqueness coming through; a worry about the past or future; an observation tinged with emotion; a reminder of what the character wants; or a change of heart after a difficult conversation. All of these ideas are available to you. Adding such layers to your work serves your premise, propels the plot, raises stakes and tension, and enriches character development. Luckily, interiority can be learned.

It's important to note that while interiority happens inside the mind, heart, and intuition of a character, their reactions can be triggered from within (internal conflict) or without (external conflict), or, often, both. For example, a plot point generates a reaction, or an inner struggle inspires the character to make a choice that changes the trajectory of the story. As we'll see later in this workbook, character and plot are interwoven like a DNA double helix.

Great interiority adds emotion and perspective to your novel or memoir, plain and simple. Instead of "He was annoyed," you open yourself up to much more interesting prose, like, "He couldn't believe that dumpster-fire-on-wheels needed fixing again. A lemon so sour, it couldn't even make lemonade." The emotion in this example is communicated to readers clearly and without explanation or condescension.

To understand this technique, think about the existence you have inside your own head. Unless you have perfected the art of mindfulness, you probably don't spend every single second perfectly embedded in the present moment. You are often "time traveling" to your memories of the past, imagined scenarios you wish had happened, or your hopes, dreams, anxieties, and fears for the future. You're constantly reliving, revising, telescoping into various possibilities, and otherwise jumping around in reality (*your* version of it, that is, as all perception is biased).

As such, our definition of interiority can be expanded to consider your character's various ideas about time—past, present, future—and the level of information they're integrating about the plot, other characters, and the story world. This is all part of being alive, so why would a protagonist's internal processes lack this type of richness and nuance? As writers, we should strive to express a character's mental and emotional world as richly as we experience our own. We can further explore interiority across four levels of narrative depth. A lot needs to be conveyed in the course of storytelling, from the most superficial ideas to the most profound. Character is the lens through which everything is channeled. Information can be deployed using four broad types of writing, and interiority is generally found at the three levels of self-expression which lie beneath simple objective statements. There are four distinct approaches to rendering information, listed from the most superficial to the deepest, as follows.

Narrative Depth: Narration

The reporting of events without reaction or interpretation, as if the character is a security camera and seeing the scene with no specific slant. Though narration is usually going to be filtered through a concrete point of view, which is inherently biased, this portrayal of events is about as neutral as you can get. Narration can be played out in a full scene, or compressed into a summary—like a progress montage in a movie. Most narration is not considered interiority.

Narrative Depth: Interpretation

Character perspective on a scene from a specific emotional or intellectual angle, with commentary and context that add a personality layer to what's being shown and experienced. Interpretation can be applied to small and big story moments to develop a character and their unique point of view. We'll mostly find interiority containing thoughts, feelings, and reactions at this level of depth.

Narrative Depth: Extrapolation

Extrapolation involves a character making meaning from scene-based stimulus. They can remember something relevant from the past, change their perception of the present or future, or decide something about the self or another character. Extrapolation is usually reserved for more pivotal moments of protagonist development, or attached to a reaction or decision which will angle the plot in a different direction due to cause-and-effect logic. In addition to being shown through thoughts, feelings, and reactions, extrapolation is closely related to setting, resetting, and analyzing expectations. At this level of narrative depth, characters can also ask questions, reexamine their positions, and otherwise dig into what a specific event, relationship, or piece of information means to them.

Narrative Depth: Subsumation

Here, a protagonist is using information or stimulus to perform self-reflection and integrate new data or emotional development into their sense of identity. Subsumation exposes something hitherto unknown about a character's subconscious and shows growth or change on a deeper level. For example, extrapolation might inspire a protagonist to take a different action, based on perception and interpretation, but subsumation might inspire a character to behave differently from a moral perspective. All five pillars of interiority can come into play at this deepest level, but extrapolation is especially relevant to inner struggle.

If we review this list, we'll notice that narration is going to almost always be present as protagonists experience scenes and move the plot along. It's crucial to acknowledge that not every moment needs interiority, as you'll see throughout this guide. Sometimes, narration is sufficient. But when we start to go deeper into character perspective with interpretation, extrapolation, and subsumation, we'll find ourselves adding different layers of connection and meaning. This is the realm of interiority.

By exploring these narrative depths, writers have the opportunity to connect with their own point of view character first, and then, eventually, foster a relationship with their audience. Basically, by using the tool of interiority, you are adding emotional context for what your character is experiencing in the moment (and, as we now realize, outside of it, too). This is key.

Interiority Text Analysis

Try to identify what kind of interiority is used, and which level of depth it conveys in the following examples.

Example 1:

The lake was pristine, shimmering in the golden late-afternoon sun. It wasn't time for fall yet. She wanted more days like this one.

Type of Interiority:

☐ Thought
☐ Feeling
☐ Reaction
☐ Expectation
☐ Inner Struggle

Level of Narrative Depth:

☐ Narration
☐ Interpretation
☐ Extrapolation
☐ Subsumation

Example 2:

The lake was pristine, shimmering in the golden late-afternoon sun. It wasn't time for fall yet. She wanted more days like this one.

Type of Interiority:

☐ Thought
☐ Feeling
☐ Reaction
☐ Expectation
☐ Inner Struggle

Level of Narrative Depth:

☐ Narration
☐ Interpretation
☐ Extrapolation
☐ Subsumation

Answer Key

While there are very few "wrong" answers in creative writing, these are my answers and rationale as a way of teaching these concepts.

Example 1:	Type of Interiority	Level of Narrative Depth
The lake was pristine, shimmering in the golden late-afternoon sun. It wasn't time for fall yet. She wanted more days like this one.	☑ Thought ☑ Feeling ☑ Reaction ☐ Expectation ☐ Inner Struggle	☑ Narration ☑ Interpretation ☐ Extrapolation ☐ Subsumation

My Take: Notice there's more than one element involved in even the most simple narration! I've selected "Interpretation" here as well because the character feels something about the landscape. This is a small moment.

Example 2:	Type of Interiority	Level of Narrative Depth
When the season changes, she'll be trapped again in her routine. In that house. It'd be so easy to keep walking and just not look back.	☑ Thought ☑ Feeling ☑ Reaction ☑ Expectation ☑ Inner Struggle	☐ Narration ☐ Interpretation ☑ Extrapolation ☑ Subsumation

My Take: Same walk but very different energy. Here, the character is extrapolating on the stimulus and no longer in the moment. Instead, she is expecting the future with trepidation and subsuming what it'll mean for her. She also has a choice to make, which pulls in inner struggle.

Nuance Across Depth Levels

We'll do many exercises as this workbook rolls on, so I'd like to call your attention to a few things early on. Notice how each bit of interiority leverages multiple mental processes. We have thoughts, feelings, and reactions in both. But in one, the character is enjoying her walk and already nostalgic about the end of summer. In another, the character brings urgency and fear to the same activity because of what she thinks will happen in the future. The second example is also pinned to plot, not just action. Should she escape rather than spend another day in her situation? Will running away fix anything? (This can be a bit of magical thinking, which we'll cover later.) Both example pieces are very short, yet both are loaded with instances of interiority which operate on different levels.

A Psychology Interlude

In terms of the human brain's function, interiority straddles the Executive Control Network (ECN) and the Default Mode Network (DMN). When your brain is using its ECN wiring, you are actively engaged, noticing, responding, considering, reacting, and experiencing intentional thought processes. When your consciousness enters the DMN, you are daydreaming, remembering, and otherwise unplugged from the present moment.

The following kinds of though processes are typical of the ECN:
- Setting and pursuing goals
- Understanding perspectives
- Communicating and being in community
- Solving problems
- Tackling obstacles

This sounds a lot like what a proactive protagonist does in storytelling. That said, you'll also want to balance this active, hard-driving ECN activation with moments spent in a DMN state, as a character retreats into their mind to remember, reflect, and subsume what events might mean. While the Executive Control Network is outward-facing, the Default Mode Network is much more inward-facing. Both have a place in our own brain-based experiences as humans, and both should feature in your character's interiority. It might be helpful for you to consider how your character thinks, how their mind works, and what audiences will experience being in their perspective. You'll notice some of these psychology concepts threaded throughout this guide, as our characters can and should be informed by real human mental patterns and processes.

And? So?

If all the technical mumbo-jumbo is a little technical for you, there are two helpful and simple questions that can also help you access deeper levels of character and interiority: "And? So?" If you find that you're having trouble getting to the bottom of your protagonist's experience, stop and ask yourself what's really going on, or how you can make additional meaning from that moment. Here's an example of how to use "And? So?" when training yourself to think more profoundly about your character's expectations, reactions, and choices. Let's say we have a scene where the protagonist, Sonia, is merely attending a work meeting before anything disruptive happens. (If nothing disruptive ever happens, of course, you may want to consider whether the scene is pulling its weight.) We'll get some narration of people filtering in, but that's not exactly story-worthy, so let's start digging.

And?
What if the big promotion gets announced at this meeting?

So?
Sonia wants it.

And?
If Sonia doesn't get it, she'll be humiliated.

So?
She'll have to save face.

And?
In front of her boss ...

So?
... who's Sonia's father.

Of course, this is exactly why Sonia probably won't get the promotion. The optics are too dicey, and both father and daughter want to avoid nepotism accusations. For this scene to really sparkle, though, Sonia should either be kept in the dark or actively misled about her chances (by Daddy himself or one of his sycophants). That way, her expectations at the beginning of the scene will generate tension and inner struggle, making the outcome seem to matter more. Notice how "And? So?" keeps us focused on continually digging deeper and raising the stakes of the situation.

At the surface narrative level, Sonia sits in a conference room, watching her colleagues get settled. But once significant events start happening, interiority kicks in to convey some of the wrinkles we just discovered with "And? So?" Interpretation should become involved, at the very least, but maybe some extrapolation and subsumation, too. Let's say she's a workaholic. Her achievements are a major part of her identity. Whatever happens with this promotion will either elevate Sonia's self-worth or plunge her into despair. There's also the potential for a twist, because success is sometimes more fraught than failure. If she does get the job, will she always wonder whether she truly earned it? Will Sonia forever have to watch her back against jealous colleagues? Are her so-called achievements even hers, or has Daddy been pulling strings behind the scenes since kindergarten? What started as a pretty normal meeting narrative can now act as an inciting incident, midpoint, act break, crisis, or climax scene (more on plot points that benefit from interiority later). If this moment ends up being pivotal, and Sonia is confronted with the loss of her job or becomes Dad's scapegoat to demonstrate a commitment to corporate fairness, she's also set up for some very interesting reactions and decisions. This hypothetical scenario brings me to a crucial question that many writers have about the logistics of interiority. When is interiority appropriate, and how much do various moments need?

How Much Interiority to Use and When?

To address this question, I like to pull out my favorite idea of the writer as a spotlight operator. Imagine a darkened theatre and a proscenium framing a stage. There's a dance number playing out, and then, suddenly ... a beam of light shines on the soloist. The audience looks there automatically. As a writer, it's your job to identify the important parts of your story. By directing reader attention to an event, impression, or interpretation, you are, in essence, shining a bright spotlight (in the form of additional interiority) and making a big statement: *Look over here! This matters!*

The more time, description, reaction, and emotion you lavish on a story element, the more a reader will believe that this thing, person, event, or idea is important. Spotlight moments in the plot are major turning points, instances of character change, events that alter the trajectory of a protagonist's objective, motivation, or need, and other places where character, plot, and the project's big-picture theme intersect. Interiority is often used to brighten and focus the spotlight at these junctures. You've gone through the trouble of creating this plot for this character. (That's right, the plot should intentionally showcase your protagonist's development.) Make the important moments more impactful with interiority and juice maximum emotion from the events you've engineered.

Another great time to use interiority is when you're establishing who your character is, their past, their present, and their imagined or expected future. No, I don't mean an info-dumping chapter of backstory right as the manuscript is trying to get off the ground.

Opening exposition is very much frowned upon in most contemporary writing that aims for traditional publication. As you get more comfortable with this tool, you can also play around with the type of interiority you use, offering superficial narration and coupling it with deeper extrapolation to enhance a moment, for example.

Sometimes great meaning can be made with a few sentences of additional insight—a dash of seasoning instead of a whole side dish. The more important the scene, the more impactful it will be to character, and the more interiority you might want to apply.

I should note that the most important instances of interiority, those at the extrapolation and subsumation levels of narrative depth, don't necessarily contribute a lot of word count to their respective stories. One idea I'll keep returning to is that our thoughts, interpretations, extrapolations, hopes, dreams, fears, etc., are specific. Instead of offering random information in interiority, you will want to develop characterizing details, which lend additional insight into the premise, theme, and, of course, protagonist.

> **Characterizing Detail:** Data that fundamentally informs a point of view protagonist's personality, objective, motivation, or reaction to stimulus, rather than irrelevant tidbits. For example, that your character's favorite movie is *Shrek* is a random fact, unless they're a champion *Shrek* cosplayer and this is crucial to your world-building and plot. On the other hand, the fact that your character only goes to watch movies in the middle of the day, when the theater is more likely to be empty, is an interesting characterizing detail. It suggests something about the character that readers have to interpret. Maybe the protagonist likes to be alone, enjoys their own company, or puts a premium on escapism. If the various attributes you're choosing for them (and which appear in their interpretations of your secondary characters) don't do some kind of double duty and deliver deeper insights, put some more thought into selecting characterizing details that do. Don't pull random preferences and facts out of a hat and call the resulting amalgamation a character.

If you think about, well, thinking, in the context of your own mental processes, you'll find that specificity makes sense. We don't often get generally nervous, unless we suffer from certain types of anxiety or experience a pervasive sense of doom. Usually, what we're afraid of is detailed and presented with context. If someone leaves a threatening message under the windshield wiper of your car one day, your mind probably won't stop at the vague question of, "Who did this?"

Instead, you might consider your longstanding enemies, as well as anybody you may have been in conflict with recently. Is this the work of your high school bully, who just got back into town? Or the woman whose parking space you accidentally stole in the Target lot the other day? You don't want to ruminate like this for pages and pages in a novel, but notice how this specificity reminds you of a more human and relatable extrapolation than the generic rhetorical question of, "Who could it be?" Specific thoughts pack more punch, too.

Obviously, detailed consideration does add to the word count. You might notice that you'll be expanding moments, rather than streamlining them, especially when you first start using interiority. However, it's entirely possible to learn the ropes, practice, and become more precise in how you use various aspects of this tool, so you're not contributing a ton of additional material with each instance. (Outside of major events that demand a bigger reaction, of course.) So far, we've defined interiority and discussed where and when to use it (in big and small moments that serve plot or character development). But missing is a sense of what, exactly, interiority looks like on the page. How do we format this stuff? Is it just italicized verbatim thought? Read on.

Formatting Interiority

There are a few set interiority formatting conventions, but their ultimate use is up to you. Like voice and writing style, interiority and its formatting are nebulous higher-order craft concepts. I want you to embrace this nebulousness, even though uncertainty can sometimes feel uncomfortable, especially when a lot of writing guides are full of set formulas and rubrics.

Interiority generally appears either folded into the narration or in italics, whether in a quiet moment of reflection or in the midst of scene and action. The first option means narrating as normal and incorporating interiority into the flow of the text itself, without any special formatting. This can work in either first or third person (more on POV in a moment). The second option renders the verbatim text of the thought, impression, reaction, or interpretation, then separates the content of that interiority with either italics or a "thought" tag. Again, this is common in both the first and third person. If we're folding the interiority into narration alongside some dialogue, it might look like this:

> "This is so yummy," she said, wondering how she might sneak away to the bathroom and spit out the gummy, flabby steak. This would be risky, and Jim would no doubt notice. What a disaster.

Using italicized verbatim thought or "thought" tags looks like:

> "Oh, so this is your favorite steak place?" she asked, forcing a smile. *Maybe the kitchen's having an off night?* But Jim seemed to be enjoying the food. *Maybe this guy's taste buds are broken*, she thought.

In the modern publishing marketplace, more writers weave interiority into the narrative without offsetting it, as we saw in the first example. However, there are still some authors who choose to use italics or "thought" tags, as demonstrated in the second example. In fact, I used italics *and* a "thought" tag, which is unusual. You can also add the "thought" tag the first few times you offer verbatim though, then let the italics formatting stand alone. This approach tends to be more common in third person, as in first person, everything the character thinks is biased and slanted through their lens, so the argument could be made that it's *all* interiority.

How you format your interiority might vary, even from project to project, though I would urge you to keep your formatting choices consistent *within* each manuscript. If you've woven interiority throughout narrative for the most part, readers might be jarred to suddenly see italicized verbatim thought and "thought" tags. The more interiority you read—or the more you start to notice it—the more you'll internalize how to use it within the flow of your own writing. It's important to note the overlap of interiority and voice here. Both rely on writing style, syntax, and word choice. By practicing one, you will always be homing in on the other.

Today's emotionally intelligent and nuanced fiction and memoir readers put a premium on getting to know your characters deeply. Interiority is your best bet for adding vulnerability and authenticity, which are huge factors that pull audiences into a story. At this turning point in our culture, when humans can be found pouring out their feelings, perspectives, and identities left and right via social media, readers want more access to a protagonist's inner life. (It's important to remember that social media shares are biased, almost always existing at the levels of interpretation, extrapolation, or subsumation.) Audiences prefer entertainment that thinks deeply and asks big questions.

At moments grand and small, today's most successful fiction and memoir authors use interiority to establish and deepen their characters. My goal is for you to notice opportunities for this in your own writing. Now that you're beginning to understand what interiority is, from the big-picture, heady concept level to the logistical how-to brass tacks, I hope you find yourself getting excited to dig in. First, let's go ahead and practice some "And? So?" on your own project. Pick a scenario you've been struggling with and let's dig in.

And? So? Questionnaire

Choose a superficial-seeming scene from your own story, one that might need extra juice, and give this technique a whirl.

The scene I'm thinking of is:

And?

So?

And?

So?

And?

So?

And?

What'd you discover doing this exercise?

Interiority Reading List

To see some of these concepts in robust action, check out these published stories with interiority-forward protagonists, separated by category.

Literary

- [ ] *Wellness* by Nathan Hill
- [ ] *Sing, Unburied, Sing* by Jesmyn Ward
- [ ] *Americanah* by Chimamanda Ngozi Adichie
- [ ] *Bad Fruit* by Ella King

Upmarket

- [ ] *Eleanor Oliphant Is Completely Fine* by Gail Honeyman
- [ ] *Amazing Grace Adams* by Fran Littlewood
- [ ] *Yellowface* by R.F. Kuang
- [ ] *Aesthetica* by Allie Rowbottom

Historical

- [ ] *The Villa* by Rachel Hawkins
- [ ] *The Underground Railroad* by Colson Whitehead
- [ ] *Homegoing* by Yaa Gyasi
- [ ] *The Vaster Wilds* by Lauren Groff
- [ ] *The Nightingale* by Kristin Hannah

Thriller

- [ ] *Everyone Here Is Lying* by Shari LaPena
- [ ] *All the Dangerous Things* by Stacey Willingham
- [ ] *The New House* by Tess Stimson

Romance and Romantic Comedy

- [ ] *Romantic Comedy* by Curtis Sittenfeld
- [ ] *Before I Let Go* by Kennedy Ryan
- [ ] *One Last Stop* by Casey McQuiston

Fantasy

- [ ] *The City We Became* by N.K. Jemisin
- [ ] *The Bear and the Nightingale* by Katherine Arden
- [ ] *Spirit Glass* by Roshani Chokshi
- [ ] *Lovecraft Country* by Matt Ruff
- [ ] *Red Queen* by Victoria Aveyard

Unique Narrative Choices

- [ ] *Brutes* by Dizz Tate
- [ ] *You* by Caroline Kepnes

Your Job as a Writer

Writing can be a private and intimate creative practice, full of experimentation and false starts. Some aspiring authors naturally want to avoid crass market talk, especially at first. I'd argue, however, that it's very important for you to know what (and why!) you're creating, the earlier the better. Especially to successfully sustain yourself through a first-draft manuscript and several rounds of revision.

Once we pivot to desiring publication, we need to take our target reader into account, perhaps for the first time. At this inflection point, I strongly believe your only job is to make that audience care. Unfortunately, most readers won't know you from Adam (yet!). They have no built-in reason to care about your book or to give up hours of their lives to read it. (In traditional publishing, this also goes for gatekeepers like literary agents and acquiring editors—you especially need to make them care if you want a shot at reaching that wider readership.)

Even well-known authors with rabid fan bases need to hook their audiences with each new book. Basically, good or bad, expert or novice, you need to earn those eyeballs. The good news is you can learn how.

How Readers Read

Readers are detectives. They want something to do when they show up to the page. The big joy of reading doesn't only come from sinking into a different world and experience, it also stems from learning, analyzing, and making judgments—in other words, engaging intentionally and critically. This means audiences want to understand how a character reveals themselves and participates in plot over the course of the story. Readers might *look* like they're just sitting there, turning pages, but they're actually playing a very active role, as our protagonists should be.

The big high of reading is the joy of discovery. By telling an eager audience a story, you are inviting their participation, empathy, time, attention, and emotional investment. Happily, a reader is already primed to give you all that, and more, but you have to know what you're doing when you say you intend to take them on a story journey.

From the jump, you'll want to develop a clever premise and hook which pique audience interest and curiosity. Of course, some reader desires will vary by genre and category, so it's important that you study the market.

Writing to Market

Your central story concept should be a foundational part of your book's design from the very beginning. (If this didn't happen prior to your current draft, that's okay. There's always revision!) When we talk about audience, book category, or genre, we're already starting to think about the kind of premise that specific readers tend to enjoy. Now, before you start to vomit, or go off on a rant about how art is *art* and there are no certain *types* of art, artists, or art appreciators, I'll tell you that I know how you're feeling. Publishing categories and genres exist, so it'd be silly to pretend otherwise.

> **Category:** You may notice that I use the terms "genre" and "category" separately and intentionally. Genre refers to a story's broad stylistic conventions and content expectations, whether it's fantasy, historical, or romance. Category refers to the target audience, such as middle grade (MG) for children ages nine to thirteen, young adult (YA) for teens ages fourteen to eighteen, or adult for anyone who has aged out of reading kidlit (though many adults still gravitate toward YA novels). It wouldn't be industry standard to call middle grade a "genre," as you can have a fantasy middle grade, or a historical middle grade, for example.

Some writers roundly reject the idea of writing to market and scoff at genre expectations, but I think these ideas are worth considering, especially if your goal is traditional publication with a Big Five house or success within a self-publishing niche. If you think you can escape these notions by publishing independently, just wait until you encounter the 4,000 different Amazon categories you'll be asked to choose from. Since this is our current reality, there's power in understanding your intended reader and, in broad strokes, what they might be looking for.

Writing to Market: This can be a somewhat controversial idea, but "writing to market" simply means crafting a story to fit perceived category desires. A classic example is the expectation of an HEA or "happily ever after" (or at least a "happy for now") ending in romance and romantic comedy. If you aim to write a mainstream genre romance for traditional or independent publication, you pretty much have to fulfill this (or have a very good reason why you don't). Your readers may not respond well otherwise. Even if you don't start out writing to market to reflect perceived trends and realities, you will want to research, understand, and pay attention to the larger publishing landscape at some point in your career (depending on your goals, of course). Writing to market isn't a requirement. Your philosophy may also change with time.

High Concept: Various publishing industry gatekeepers often express a preference for "high concept" projects. This means that the premise is easily expressed, and the ensuing story does exactly what it says on the box. Imagine the type of narrative that often gets made into a movie. A kid is left home alone for the holidays (the *Home Alone* franchise). Dinosaurs are resurrected from DNA samples for entertainment, until this backfires (the *Jurassic Park* franchise). The idea doesn't require nuanced explanation for someone to "get it." Compare this to "a newly single parent comes to terms with life." The latter is not necessarily a bad story, it's just not a high-concept one. A lot of action and adventure narrative, fantasies, thrillers, and romcoms get the high concept label, but this description can apply within any genre and category.

As you think about your premise and intended audience—whether that's fans of historical military fiction, self-help junkies for your memoir of resilience and redemption, or kids ages nine to twelve for your sweet coming-of-age novel helmed by a plucky young protagonist—you can acknowledge that all readers have tastes, and those tastes make them engage with certain ideas more favorably than others.

More importantly, once you understand your audience, you might have a leg up in making your characters more relatable to them. Not perfect, not even consistently sympathetic, but relatable.

Character Relatability

Character introductions always stress writers out, even memoir writers, who theoretically know their protagonists inside and out. That's because the all-important first meeting between the reader and protagonist has to be artfully done. Gone are the days of, "Hi, my name is Ruby. I'm in middle management, and my favorite outside-of-work hobby is birdwatching." Sorry. This kind of direct exposition is distinctly out of style, and it's also telling about the core essence of your character, which is, indeed, the kind of telling your English teacher warned you about (as we'll see toward the end of this chapter). When you introduce your protagonist, prioritize relatability over demographic data.

> **Relatability:** A protagonist quality designed to engender reader empathy, connection, and a sense of commonality between the character and audience. Relatability arises from a number of choices that writers make, like giving the protagonist recognizable flaws and foibles, vulnerabilities and values, driving wants and needs, specific characterizing details and quirks that are observed from real life, or any combination of these. The goal is to get readers to care about the protagonist, even if the character doesn't always make the right choices or isn't consistently sympathetic.

Today's savvy audiences are more interested in the big questions. What is a character's ... well, character? What's their sense of purpose? Which roles do they play in their life and world, and do they accept or reject these?

What "kind of person" do they feel they are, and who might they want to be, if they're still evolving? These are the types of things that you should be thinking about as you design your point-of-view protagonist.

The keys to inspiring relatability and reader connection are multifold. My first warning here is to avoid trying to create someone "everyone" will like. As contemporary storytelling craft and style have emerged, writers are capturing audiences by keenly observing human mannerisms, foibles, and behaviors. One of my favorite experiences as a reader happens when a small thought, reaction, interpretation, or impulse displayed by a character in action or interiority rings so true that I feel a surprising kinship with them. Other people think and feel this way? I'm not alone? This type of connection is the gold you're digging for.

Even if a character is inherently different from their reader, it's still possible for opposites to attract. Especially if the writer has taken pains to fully render the protagonist, define their value system, empower them with specific wants and needs, offer a peek at formative and emotional backstory, and raise the stakes so the present journey matters. It's also a good idea to make a character fundamentally good inside, even if they are flawed, make mistakes, have shaky self-worth, or seem damaged or unhinged. Their good and valiant qualities should generally outnumber the negative ones, but perfection is not expected. The best and easiest way to get readers on board with a character is by showing audiences what they care about.

Many relatable characters also operate with misbeliefs or self-doubts that readers can empathize with. In order to write interiority and authentically connect with audiences, writers aspiring to create intelligent, relatable, and consumable fiction for the contemporary market need to get very comfortable with emotion and vulnerability—their characters' *and* their own. By feeling deeply first, you can access a protagonist deeply enough to convey your themes and ideas to others. So prepare to go on a personal journey, even as you're plumbing the depths of a fictional person. You should also expect to put your character into action early—and keep them there throughout the story. Creating a proactive protagonist goes a long way to compelling readers into turning pages.

Proactive Protagonists

At the center of every good story is a relatable character who's hard at work doing … something. Actually, *what* they're doing doesn't matter nearly as much as the fact they're doing it in the first place. They don't even have to do it successfully! In fact, they can fail in small or major ways throughout your plot, and all of this will add to their perceived charm. Readers love a proactive protagonist. Ideally, this go-getter quality will propel your character throughout the entire narrative, because there's nothing worse than a "character-driven" story that's not driven by character at all.

> **Proactive Protagonist:** A protagonist who pursues internal and external objectives and needs over the course of a story. Even if yours is primarily a plot-driven novel, like a thriller, or a memoir where you're stringing together seemingly unrelated events into a cohesive structure, there should be a sense that the character is in forward motion toward one or several goals, from scene to scene, and act to act. While characters can and should react to external conflict at times, their primary progress through the story must aim toward the realization of their small and large goals. Interiority is used to add cause-and-effect logic and create stakes, tension, and growth. With a proactive protagonist, plot is steered and affected by decisions they make.

The reason readers attach to a proactive protagonist has a lot to do with audiences and their real lives (which they are fleeing to spend time in books). Many modern readers may feel out of control in between bouts of doom-scrolling and sagging under the burdens of their non-reading responsibilities. As a result, they might dream of inhabiting the consciousness of kick-ass heroes who aren't quite so constrained. Writers themselves can absolutely relate to these feelings, with the relative loss of control inherent in the publishing process. Why not add a healthy dose of aspirational wish fulfillment as you design your characters and premises?

Remember that readers want to care. But they also want to live vicariously through larger-than-life events elevated into something meaningful. Even though reactive/passive protagonists can be relatable and realistic, your goal is to aim higher. Find ways to put your character into the driver's seat in a way that fits within the parameters of the story. The goal is a protagonist who makes the plot happen, rather than letting it happen to them.

Put your character into proactive action from the very first pages of your story, whether you knock them down or show them climbing. Why? Because both failing and striving are incredibly relatable. To round out this section, I'll challenge a perfectly well-meaning and pervasive piece of writing advice. The familiar paradigm of "show, don't tell" has been wrecking prose and making writers nervous for centuries. Instead, it's better to use an expert combination of showing and telling, and this is my hill to die on. Interiority occupies the gray area between these approaches.

It's Okay to Show and Tell

The old craft chestnut of "show, don't tell" has some wisdom behind it. But since it's considered Writing 101, many writers follow it blindly without digging any deeper. This is a mistake. There are actually multiple types of telling. That's right, not all telling is created equal.

Many writers already know that "telling" simply means stating emotion, objective, motivation, characterization, etc., in the text itself. Think, "She was angry," and, "He is a nice guy, the kind who'd give a buddy the shirt off his back." Meanwhile, "showing" is the practice of demonstrating some of these same ideas, emotions, and character traits through action. Think, "She balled her fists up into tight knots," and the narrative description of the character giving someone the shirt off his literal back.

> **Telling:** Explicit statements of story and character realities, where the author or narrator speaks directly to the reader in an expository or explanatory manner. This gets in the way of reader extrapolation and discovery by overtly expressing thematic, character, and plot elements. There is wisdom to the advice of "show, don't tell," which steers writers away from passive telling, but some telling is appropriate and warranted, as long as it occurs in concert with showing and leaves room for audiences to participate.

Showing: An action-based method of displaying a character's inner life via external means, from dialogue to movement to the sensation in their physical body. This allows readers to play along by interpreting what's happening below the surface and extrapolating why. It also reminds writers to keep their stories active with narrative and scene. But if you're only showing throughout your story, this approach can present some unique challenges and get in the way of deeper character exploration.

Think of our detective readers, who like to be actively involved in uncovering and interpreting information. If you simply tell them everything you want them to know, you risk them feeling like outsiders with no stake in the story. "She was angry" might be true and clear, but it doesn't ask anything of the audience. It's disposable information that doesn't elicit empathy, either. Reading the word "angry" won't make me feel angry (though the flagrant emotional telling might!). It won't even make me think, and that's the issue.

Contrast "She was angry" with, "If that no-good, rotten jerk ever darkens my doorstep again, I'll knock him into next Thursday." This communicates anger in a colorful and engaging way, using interiority and voice. It lets the reader draw the connection between the prose and the emotion of "angry."

Leaving an opening for interpretation invites the audience to reach out, emote, and relate to a character's feelings. As a result, readers take personal ownership of the storytelling process, which is key. Below are some derivative examples of showing and telling, intended to make a point.

Showing and Telling Text Analysis

Each idea gets two incarnations in the examples below—one, telling, one, showing.

| He was angry. | ☐ Showing ☐ Telling |
| He huffed and slammed the door. | ☐ Showing ☐ Telling |

She was nervous.	☐ Showing	☐ Telling
Her stomach fluttered with butterflies.	☐ Showing	☐ Telling
She fell head over heels in love.	☐ Showing	☐ Telling
Her heart hammered in her chest.	☐ Showing	☐ Telling
He was nice.	☐ Showing	☐ Telling
He pulled the cat out of the storm drain.	☐ Showing	☐ Telling
The house had a creepy vibe.	☐ Showing	☐ Telling
The floorboards groaned beneath their feet.	☐ Showing	☐ Telling
She was very smart.	☐ Showing	☐ Telling
She had the answer before Bill could pull out his calculator.	☐ Showing	☐ Telling

He was nice.	☐ Showing	☑ Telling
He pulled the cat out of the storm drain.	☑ Showing	☐ Telling
The house had a creepy vibe.	☐ Showing	☑ Telling
The floorboards groaned beneath their feet.	☑ Showing	☐ Telling
She was very smart.	☐ Showing	☑ Telling
She had the answer before Bill could pull out his calculator.	☑ Showing	☐ Telling

Why This Matters

Telling, at its core, is incredibly condescending. It doesn't trust the reader to do their job—and in the case of most people who actively choose to be readers, it's a job they love. Egregious telling in a manuscript feels like a pat on the head. It also (perhaps unintentionally) communicates a lack of writing confidence. It's as if the writer doesn't think they've done a good job of making the story speak for itself. You shouldn't approach your reader relationship from this place of insecurity. I know, I know, that's easier said than done. But once you realize that you don't have to explain, you can trust yourself to tell the story and trust your reader to follow. It's a terrifying and liberating breakthrough, and something I hope you experience as you start applying the concepts in this guide to your own work.

But here's where things get more nuanced: The simple "show, don't tell" dichotomy doesn't give writers or readers the full story. If you unlearn what you think you know about this advice, you might start noticing telling all over published books. Has there been some kind of massive error? Does publishing have a huge double standard, enabling a shady cabal of writers who are "allowed" to tell? No. Because there are multiple types of telling, and not all are bad. In fact, some are downright necessary. This is where I draw a distinction between what I call "bad telling" and "good telling."

First, let's discuss bad telling and the writing elements you should avoid simply telling about:

- Inherent Personality Traits
  - Don't outright explain personality traits that are central to your character's core identity, whether the protagonist is a "good sport" or a "loose cannon."
- Emotions
  - When readers hear that someone is "hurt" or "sad" or even "happy," this is the most superficial expression of an emotion. The "why" behind a feeling is almost always more interesting than the feeling itself, which is either provided in context within the scene or communicated using interiority. There's also the thought that triggers the feeling, and its aftermath. None of these juicy ideas can be explored if you're merely labeling the emotion.

Here's an example:

> Tina was a loyal person, but this latest fight had hurt her very badly. James had been her friend since the second grade, and Tina didn't want to jeopardize such a longstanding and meaningful relationship. Still, she found herself undecided.

This is straightforward bad telling. It delivers information but there's no sense of voice or emotional inflection. You'll notice that "hurt" and "undecided" don't really do much justice to the betrayal that Tina might be feeling. The information lies on the page like roadkill on the turnpike.

Contrast it with the following.

> She wanted to hate James, everyone said she should. But Tina couldn't throw away eleven years of friendship. Could she?

Not only are the ideas of "hurt" and "undecided" communicated with more nuance—as the reader must work to unearth them from the prose—but we get information about the length of the friendship in context. Thanks to interiority, the data is seamlessly inserted without calling much overt attention to itself. This second example involves good telling, which you may not have felt comfortable exploring before. Certain categories of information can and should be conveyed with interiority and narration. Sometimes, there's really no good way to say it … except to say it. The below story elements fit under the good telling umbrella:

- Backstory
  - What are some significant past events that have shaped a character, for better or worse (or both)?
- Context
  - What's happening for your character in their current place in their growth arc and the overall plot? Why is it important?
- Objective
  - What does the character want and why do they want it?
- Self-Perception
  - How does the protagonist see themselves? Is this in conflict with anything or anyone else? Does their self-perception change as they go through the story? Do they shift from their objective to their need, and what are the ramifications of this transition?
- Inner Struggle
  - What's the biggest thing they're grappling with, on a personal level (in general) or in difficult times (in particular)?
- Plot Tension and Conflict
  - What are the story's sources of external, plot-based conflict?
- Stakes
  - What are the consequences of a specific event or choice? What happens if the character is successful or unsuccessful in a present or future action?
- World-building
  - If you're writing in a speculative, fantasy, science fiction, or historical genre, you'll want to include details about the world or era, why it works the way it does, and how these issues affect character development and plot.

You might start to recognize that a lot of these story elements intersect with the broader definition of interiority. Yep, that's right. Interiority is good telling. I often find myself writing *"Interiority instead!"* in the margins of client manuscripts, especially when I notice too much showing (or bad telling). There's certain information that's difficult to transmit to readers without it being explicitly stated *somewhere*. Funnily enough, the writers who are showing too much—doing the "right" type of writing!—are sometimes struggling the most in the interiority department. Their characters display the same cluster of physical clichés for emotion— hammering hearts, stomach butterflies, white-knuckle fingers on steering wheels—over and over, with no deeper insights for readers to explore.

A major benefit of strong interiority is its ability to provide seamless context. Writers often struggle with establishing information and backstory. It can be tough to draw the line between good and bad telling. They know that a character needs extra dimension but are often unsure how to provide it without hitting readers over the head. Interiority is an elegant way to deploy not only emotion but information, and offer reasons why both matter. So if you keep a wreath of Post-its around your computer monitor, or reminders above your writing desk, you might want to add the soon-to-be-second-nature comment and questions of "Interiority instead!" and "And? So?" to your vision board.

INTERIORITY
INSTEAD!
AND? SO?

The point is simple. I don't really care that a character is crying. Tears shown on someone's face aren't going to make me commiserate. I also especially don't care *that* a character is merely thinking. This is a big one. "Thoughts whirled around in her head." Okay. That's nice. Anything more specific? And? So?

Intention is key. Characters are individuals. Everyone experiences emotions and events differently. When I'm sad, I might look like I'm hungry (because I'm eating so much junk food). When you're sad, it might look like you're angry (because you're pounding the wall). If you're only showing those external actions, a whole layer is missing.

Relying on the visual presentation of an emotion leaves no room for nuance. Why is the character crying? What's the thought that touched off the tears? We all know what it's like to be overcome with emotion, but it's often a very specific thought or image that sparks the waterworks. The physical body can only tell us so much. Then we have to dig deeper. Your character isn't a mime.

This is why interiority transcends the limitations of both telling and showing, and why it's such a crucial tool to add to your ever-expanding understanding of writing and storytelling. Though many of you are grown-ass adults and don't need anyone's permission to do anything, I'll give it anyway: It's okay to both show *and* tell, as long as you focus on good telling. Just in case this helps you feel more comfortable.

On the following pages, let's lay the groundwork of your character and target audience. Then we'll discuss premise and theme.

Protagonist Basics Questionnaire

I am writing a:

- [ ] Novel
- [ ] Memoir
- [ ] Narrative nonfiction project

My story has:

- [ ] One main protagonist
- [ ] Multiple protagonists (or multiple POVs)

What inspired me to write this story?

Who is my target audience?

What is my protagonist's sense of purpose?

Which roles does my character play in their life and world, and do they accept or reject these?

What "kind of person" do they feel they are, and who might they want to be, if they're still evolving?

What are some of their flaws, foibles, and misbeliefs? (We'll get into this in a lot more detail later.)

What makes my primary protagonist relatable?

Why will my audience connect with them?

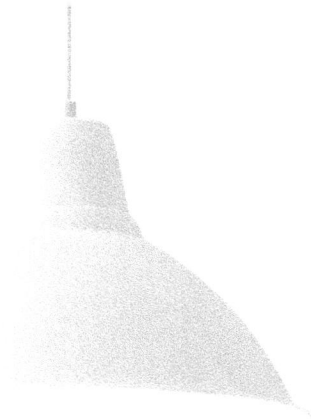

Premise and Theme

Before we get into the deep work of character development, let's talk about the story that's going to support your protagonist and plot. A lot of narratives have several interconnected ideas operating behind the scenes. Together these can be called theme and premise. In practice, theme often supports the early story concept and its evolution, while premise is the audience-facing expression of your idea, which is more relevant during the revision and pitching processes.

> **Theme:** The "core emotional experience" of the story, or what it's about on an implicit, human level. This is the topic, assertion, or argument that you keep at the front of your mind while writing and that you want your audience to consider while reading. Though the theme is ever-present in a story, it's rarely stated outright.

> **Premise:** This is the audience-facing, explicit explanation of your story that can pull together character, plot, and theme. For the purpose of this guide, I generally use "premise" to mean a short summary of your main character and plot points. In the larger publishing industry, it can also refer to a formal elevator pitch or logline statement that's used to succinctly present a manuscript or published book.

The fact is, stories are all about something, whether a clever premise or a protagonist's emotional growth arc. Memoirs also have a theme, or at least they should. A life story from the cradle to the present day is an autobiography, and these can be extremely hard to sell to traditional publishers unless you're a household name. The overwhelming majority of contemporary memoirs encapsulate events and reflections around a specific idea—love after loss, triumph over adversity, a unique family dynamic, etc.—which helps writers be selective with their focus when shaping a narrative from millions of lived experiences.

While you should be specific with your premise, you don't want to pressure yourself to create something singular. There are no new stories to tell. At some point in recorded or forgotten history, someone has probably played with similar characters, plot points, and ideas. There are many familiar notions floating around in brains and slush piles; on hard drives and shelves. There are only so many different types of clay in the world but look at the incredible variety of pottery that comes from the imaginations and hands of individual creators. You may not win solely on your book idea. Instead, you might win on your character, writing style, and interiority.

> **Idea-Execution Dichotomy:** The theme, premise, and idea constitute just one part of a novel or memoir. It's notable that you can't copyright a book idea. The execution—how that idea is expressed and explored on the page—is where you can really leave your mark. And that's what we copyright: the words that comprise the written work itself. Successful novels and memoirs combine both a good, relatable, and interesting idea that's likely to resonate with their target audiences, and an execution that demonstrates intentional writing craft on every page.

Each writer is capable of creating a specific and nuanced character, and *they* can be your unique selling proposition. Other writers may be working with a similar premise to yours right now, but only you are capable of giving it your spin.

Developing Theme and Premise

To that end, you will want to answer the following question as soon as possible, ideally before you sit down to draft: What's your story about? Be specific. It's also helpful to know who your intended audience is and which thematic ideas you're hoping to explore. This helps to set up the character's growth arc, as audiences can understand the protagonist's early worldview and intuit how far they have to go to realize a more evolved outlook. From there, explorations of the theme and premise appear throughout. These elements reinforce the book's essence to the writer, at first, then to agents and other publishing gatekeepers, and finally, to readers. I strongly suggest that you get clear on these major ideas—even if you don't have all of your plot ingredients and narrative choices hammered out yet—because your ideation, writing, revision, and pitching process will be easier. When you're designing the premise of your story and thinking about your plot, consider what might be engaging and aspirational about it. That's the "promise of the premise."

> **Promise of the Premise:** This depends on your genre, audience expectations, and story idea. You'll want to develop storytelling sequences that show off the unique attributes of your novel or memoir and which will plunge your readers more deeply into your particular idea. Think of what's aspirational, inspirational, or noteworthy about your premise, then play it up with your settings, plot obstacles, and how "big" you let your protagonist go in the pursuit of their objective and need. Even ordinary characters and lives can offer fun sequences of wish-fulfillment or high emotional stakes. What kinds of scenarios and experiences are only available in your story world and to your particular protagonist?

If you're writing something that can be considered dark academia, for example, you'll want to offer plot and character elements which live up to the promise of the premise. This means protagonists who stay up all night falling in love or debating big ideas, parties in secret chambers, hushed libraries with soaring ceilings, new best friends, fresh foes, and an atmosphere of extreme academic and social pressure that promises either acceptance or bitter rejection. One of the worst outcomes for a young person in this kind of environment is to feel irrelevant. The stakes are high, especially if you're weaving in speculative or fantasy elements, and this is exactly what a dark academia audience will be drawn to.

Ideally, you've come up with a good novel idea that will showcase an exciting sequence of events, or lived some interesting experiences that can become a memoir. Show these off and have fun! Figure the theme out, then use it as your North Star while drafting and revising. It's actually quite easy to boil down the essence of a story, as long as you've arrived at that clarity in your own mind first. The following exercises will help you do just that.

Premise and Theme Questionnaire

What's your story about (your premise)? Be specific.

Which thematic ideas are you hoping to explore?

State your theme:

What's the promise of your premise?

Premise Text Analysis

Premise isn't always present in every line of a manuscript, but there are times when premise shows up in interiority and reflects deeper thematic elements. Below, extrapolate what each example's theme or premise might be.

> This character senses an intruder in her household.

Example 1:
In my child-like mind, I believed that if I could only get rid of her new husband, things would go back to the way they were. She would simply be my mother again, just the two of us against the world.

These are the theme and premise ideas involved:

_____

_____

_____

> **My Take**: This is a great example of objective, motivation, and need. On the theme level, I'd say that "coming of age" comes to the forefront in this interiority. We also get a sense of the character's desperation for "things [to] go back to the way they were," though she seems to realize that her desires are part of her "child-like mind" and, as a result, unreasonable.

43

Sharpen your previous theme/premise statement (if you want):

_____

_____

_____

This fantasy character resents being "handled" in a hostile new kingdom.

Example 2:

He scrutinized the withered face of his servant. Why send such a frail woman to mind him? He could snap her like a twig without breaking a sweat.

"Oh, don't scowl, little lamb," the matronly woman said, reaching up to pinch his cheek. And, suddenly, he was five years old again, everything he'd done since leaving home erased with one surprising touch.

These are the theme and premise ideas involved:

_____

_____

_____

My Take: Here, we have a clash between a character's external presentation or demeanor and his inner need. Thematically, we can expect some power struggle, as well as the revelation of inner vulnerability for this character. On a plot and premise level, this protagonist, it seems, must grapple with what they've done "since leaving home."

Sharpen your previous theme/premise statement (if you want):

_____

_____

_____

A fantasy being expects this character to change base metals to gold

Example 3:
He presented yet another assignment for my inspection, the metal jingling like shackles.

These are the theme and premise ideas involved:

_____

_____

_____

My Take: This is a very elegant way to convey the character's bind with the image of "shackles" to refer to both the literal metal the antagonist is offering and to suggest the protagonist's sense of being trapped.

Sharpen your previous theme/premise statement (if you want):

_____

_____

_____

Premise and Theme Checklist

01 My theme is clear to me as the implied idea of what the story is about.

YES ☐ NO ☐

02 If I'm layering multiple themes onto the project, they are related and will result in a story that feels cohesive.

YES ☐ NO ☐

03 I'll remember to use my thematic idea to stay focused while drafting.

YES ☐ NO ☐

04 I'll also remember to use my thematic idea to check my manuscript for cohesiveness while revising.

YES ☐ NO ☐

05 I've tried to express the major story elements as a premise statement. This includes:

☐ Character

☐ Main plot point, climax, or resolution

☐ Theme

Write it here:

Point of View and·Plot

Interiority is inherently tied to the concept of point of view. If you've been intuitively feeling your way around POV in your writing without making conscious choices, this could be a mistake. The more intentional your use of point of view, the clearer your storytelling. Within the confines of perspective, you'll find great control and order. Sometimes, creative constraints actually illuminate a clear path forward. Point of view is one such craft element.

> **Point of View:** If your novel is a movie, the POV is the camera lens that's recording the action and conveying a sense of narrative distance that separates the reader from the story. Is the audience inside a primary character's head, as close as possible ("first person")? Is the camera zoomed out a bit, but with access to one character's inner life ("close third person" or "third-person limited")? Or does the camera zoom around above the action, able to see and know all ("omniscient")? Multiple POV, where different sections or chapters are told from distinct perspectives (with each character written in either first or third) is also an option.

Let's discuss your generally available point-of-view options in more detail.

First-person POV

The preferred perspective for certain categories, like children's books, memoir, and some upmarket. The obvious benefit of first-person POV is that readers get immediate access to your character with very little narrative distance, which engenders closeness and connection. It can also help writers get into their protagonist's mindset and experiences more easily. However, you're also locked into your character's perspective in first, with no way to separate the narrative from a protagonist's experience. If you need to reveal information to the reader but not the character—say in a thriller or mystery novel—you're out of luck.

> **Narrative Distance:** Also sometimes called "psychic distance." Compare the view from inside your specific brain to the perspective a deity might have, floating above their charges and observing. The "narrative distance" is much closer to the action in the first instance than it is in the second, especially if the deity doesn't have access to individual perspectives. The current novel and memoir market prefers closer narrative distance, while the omniscient point of view, which offers greater distance, is considered more outdated or specialized. You can always bridge the narrative distance gap and access your characters on a deeper level with interiority. Writers using third person close or omniscient might find they need to work harder to overcome narrative distance and stay attuned to their POV characters' experiences.

Close Third-person POV

This is also very popular, especially in genre and literary fiction, and a lot of agents and publishers are actively seeking well-executed examples. In this POV, the camera follows your protagonist closely but can also break away and "zoom out" onto other action. We're observing the protagonist "outside in" instead of "inside out" (as in first person). When you go into the third person, you have to work harder to grant the reader access to your POV and close the narrative distance. As such, interiority becomes more important.

Omniscient Third-person POV

This is quite difficult to do and requires substantial focus and intentionality. Certain categories—like high fantasy, hard sci-fi, some thriller, and literary fiction—lend themselves well to this narrative choice. In its wildest form, this POV allows the camera to wander around in the action, potentially diving into any character perspective the writer sees fit. One of the benefits of omniscient is the ability to create a really strong narrative voice, a writing style that almost becomes a separate character in and of itself.

Multiple POVs

You can also experiment with more than one chronology and multiple point-of-view protagonists. If advanced narrative technique is calling you, know that the market very much prefers a multiple-POV project with a more organized approach. This can mean entire sections or, more commonly, chapters told in either first or third person as you follow various characters around. The divide between POVs is neat and orderly, and the reader never feels confused, unless that's your intended effect, of course. The benefit of multiple POVs and chronologies is that you can play with different styles of storytelling and do a lot of neat plot tricks, like ending on a cliffhanger in one character's POV, then zooming away to unrelated action, all while keeping both threads taut with various curiosity hooks working simultaneously.

> **Curiosity Hooks:** Small mysteries or questions which can also be called "open loops" and will mostly be resolved over the course of the plot. The purpose is to keep readers curious, unsettled, or unsatisfied (in this case, a good thing!). When an outstanding question is answered, we "close the loop." Expert writers never stop opening new loops or planting hooks (especially in a series idea) so there's always at least one dangling carrot enticing readers forward at all times.

One common question I get from writers working with multiple POVs is: How do I choose which character "owns" the perspective in a particular moment? Easy. Consider who has the most dynamic emotional experience in the scene at hand, who stands to gain or lose the most, who's doggedly pursuing an objective or need, or who's poised at a big turning point—internally, externally, or both. They should probably be your main perspective.

Head-hopping

Something called "head-hopping" tends to happen if you give multiple characters point-of-view access in one scene without delineating between POVs with section or chapter breaks, and this can become needlessly complicated. I strongly recommend structurally separating each perspective, especially if you're trying multiple points of view for the first time. This will also allow you to close the narrative distance on your point-of-view character in a particular section and sink more deeply into their experience. If you're constrained to one protagonist's POV at a time, you're more likely to explore it fully.

If you have multiple POV characters who are present for an event, you don't want to show the same scene from each perspective. Sure, each individual character might be experiencing something new, but readers have seen the given moment play out before. Whenever you repeat an event or a piece of information, remember what audiences already know. Trust them to retain what they've learned. Instead of repeating, add layers, nuance, data, or make fresh meaning from the plot.

Working with Tense

Tense is another decision writers must make for each project, but your options are very straightforward: past or present. (Future tense exists but isn't usually used for an entire project.) Some writers gravitate to one or the other tense naturally, while others prefer to match tense to the character or plot at hand. When you consider which tense to use, think about how well it might play with the POV you've chosen. You have the in-your-face immediacy of first-person present and the more removed third-person past. What kind of effect are you trying to achieve? What do readers expect?

Tense: Your two main options are past tense ("I ran") and present tense ("I run"). Both can be used across all available POVs. Present tense tends to bring immediacy and tension to the narrative, while past tense can feel more contemplative or even-keel and is considered the classic choice.

Each tense has its pitfalls. First-person present tense can be exhausting, especially when paired with a brisk plot. When combined with an especially slow or nonexistent structure, it can create an odd dissonance. Present tense can also generate a flurry of "-ing" verbs, or present participles, which can become grating to read. When you go further into past action in the past tense via a flashback, for example, you might fall into the dreaded past-perfect verb trap, or the "had had." This does awful things for voice, and I suggest being very clear in your chronological transitions, then continuing in normal past tense, as usual, for the flashback material itself.

Starting Your Story

The first few pages of a novel or memoir are often the most anxiety-provoking passages on any writer's to-do list. A lot is expected from the opening of a book-length project. At the very beginning of a novel—and here, I'm talking about the first few words—there's a skewed power dynamic. The writer has *all* of the information, the reader has none.

Unfortunately, the writer can't just shovel a bunch of data onto the page as if they're lecturing to a captive audience—simply because the audience isn't captive just yet. While the premise is, in and of itself, a hook, the burden to bear it out in action falls on your opening page, then chapter, then first act. This is the most critical spot in the manuscript and your only job is to **make your reader care**.

While this workbook isn't a guide on first pages or chapters, I do recommend these best practices:
- Offer access to your main point-of-view protagonist right away, ideally as they're doing something relatable, interesting, or jarring (depending on your genre). Start in scene, with dialogue, action, and some smaller-scale tension.

- Suggest or express your theme in a covert way so readers know what—in the broadest possible terms—they'll be reading "about."
- Open some loops and embed some hooks, which can be as simple as an intriguing envelope arriving with no postmark; the question of who the character should take to prom; or a reference to a past event that seems so dramatic that readers will immediately want the scoop.
- Avoid using a prologue unless you absolutely need one. These can read as a high-stakes bait and switch, especially if the real the first chapter feels like a giant energetic comedown.

Even if you don't start your story with a big-bang event-based introduction to the project's main themes and ideas, you should know what those are and express them overtly or covertly in the opening chapters. As you plan your beginning, your character will ideally already be in turmoil. Interiority is very helpful in conveying this. Even though your opening introduces plot, which is happening outside your character, you get to play with their thoughts about, expectations for, interpretations of, and reactions to the early events of your story. These should also introduce conflict and tension.

Conflict: Any fiction and memoir event, character relationship, inner struggle, or obstacle which translates to difficulty for the protagonist. It can be internal or external, as small as a paper cut and as large as the decision to take a dystopian society down from within. Conflict often involves uncomfortable growth or pain, frustrated objectives, unmet needs, and, of course, physical pain or harm stemming from external action. Conflict generally gains meaning and resonance from stakes.

Tension: Tension is the gas in your story engine and keeps readers engaged. You don't just need conflict in your story. You must also use interiority to underscore why certain obstacles and struggles matter to your character on a deeper level. Conflict generates a sense of tension within a protagonist (and for readers) as the hero grapples with internal or external issues and proactively works toward something which will bring them back to equilibrium or resolve the problem at hand. Tension applies at the scene level and across the larger plot. All conflict creates tension, but not all tension involves outright conflict.

The Seven Plot Tentpoles

Your plot will ideally be structured to generate maximum conflict and tension for your main character. Here, I'll offer seven specific sequences you can focus on developing for your story.

Tentpole: Inciting Incident

An event early in the plot that ramps up stakes and gets readers invested in the character and story. The first major conflict in your structure, the inciting incident changes the character's status from "normal" to "abnormal" in a way that creates tension which they—and the reader—become invested in resolving.

Tentpole: Escalating Obstacles

This is a large swath of the plot that covers parts of the first and second acts, if you're working with a traditional three-act structure. It's the gradual yet steady slide into despair as your character attempts to achieve their objective, fails, realizes they have growth to do, struggles with said growth, grapples with their vulnerability, and otherwise goes from confident to insecure. This section strips away their hopes that the solution to their conflict will come to them quickly and easily, or that they'll be able to succeed without changing or sacrificing some of the personal misbeliefs and qualities that brought them to conflict's doorstep in the first place.

Tentpole: Midpoint

The midpoint is when pretensions and illusions fall away and the true nature of the plot's conflict and the protagonist's vulnerability is revealed. The character goes from "solving the problem the wrong way" by relying on their limited understanding of their sense of self and the story they're in, to digging down deep and steeling themselves to "solve the problem the right way" in the second half, as conflicts and stakes escalate toward the climax. The midpoint requires humility and courage in equal parts, and this is where the protagonist starts to truly become a "hero worthy of their story."

Tentpole: Crisis

There's often an "Act II crisis" in story structure where a character is truly tested before they're cleared for the final climax. This is like a run-up to the climactic action, where things hang in the balance but the character flounders or doubts themselves, going back to old patterns and not quite nailing the transition from pursuing their want to going after their need.

Tentpole: Dark Night of the Soul

Tension is highest leading up to this character development point, which generally precedes or coincides with the climax. As the protagonist approaches the most high-stakes and dangerous (physically, emotionally, or both) moment in the story, they take stock. This is a final test they must overcome from within—their last chance to either back out or commit.

Tentpole: Synthesis Climax

The protagonist just did deep inquiry and resolved to give the conflict their all. Now, they're surprised to learn that they can actually triumph by marshaling what they've learned or leaning into what was once perceived as their weakness. They synthesize the virtuous and problematic parts of themselves to claim plot victory or, at the very least, a new level of selfhood that they never would've achieved otherwise. If this sounds like a cheesy "the magic was inside them all along" moral, that's actually spot on. This tentpole moment is all about the character realizing that they are enough during the most dire circumstances of your plot.

Tentpole: Ending

In most instances, your character will eventually triumph. They'll sacrifice, suffer losses, and reach deeper into themselves than ever before, but they will triumph. If they don't, you are technically writing a tragedy, and that's all fine and good, as long as this ending is intentional.

The final image of your project generally echoes the beginning, comes full circle, or reverses expectations. It also creates a sense of how the protagonist might move forward in the short- and medium-term in the reader's mind. Your character will have other conflicts, they will still fail and flounder, but once they've achieved synthesis, solved the present conflict, and somewhat resolved their need and wound, they're much better prepared for anything else the future brings. If engineered well, the climax and ending bring everything together, and all of the turbulence and trouble a writer has created for their protagonist seems worth it to both character and reader. Goals are realized (or not), stakes come to pass (or don't), relationships are ironed out (for the most part), and the protagonist reaches a new level of mastery or understanding of themselves and their lives. The inner struggle crests and resolves (maybe in unexpected ways), and readers leave more or less emotionally satisfied (even if you're planning a series).

These are obviously broad strokes examples of how these tentpole moments relate to character, and I've written them to be widely applicable. Plot is the crucible in which your protagonist confronts not only external tensions and conflicts, but internal ones, too. What they do and how they do it matters, but so does who they are and who they become. Now let's cement our understanding of POV, tense, and plot with some exercises, worksheets, questionnaires, and a bonus reading list.

POV and Tense Checklist

I know the point of view I'm writing in.

01
- [ ] First-person POV
- [ ] Close-third POV
- [ ] Omniscient third POV
- [ ] Multiple styles for multiple narrators

YES [ ] NO [ ]

02 If I'm writing in first-person, I understand that there is no way to separate the narrative from a protagonist's experience.   YES ☐   NO ☐

03 If I'm writing a story with multiple POVs, each voice is distinct. I can flip to a random page and know exactly which POV I'm in.   YES ☐   NO ☐

04 If I'm writing a story with multiple POVs, I don't show the same scene from each perspective, unless the replay adds fresh meaning to the plot.   YES ☐   NO ☐

05 I know the tense I'm writing in.   YES ☐   NO ☐

    ☐ Past tense ("I ran")

    ☐ Present tense ("I run")

06 I understand how to avoid the potential issues with my chosen tense.   YES ☐   NO ☐

Multi-POV Reading List

If you want to see your options for multiple POVs and explore various narrative structures that take advantage of bringing more than one perspective or timeline to the table, check out the following titles.

☐ *The New House* by Tess Stimson

☐ *Spinning Silver* by Naomi Novik

☐ *Before I Let Go* by Kennedy Ryan

- [ ] *Wellness* by Nathan Hill

- [ ] *Lovecraft Country* by Matt Ruff

- [ ] *The Villa* by Rachel Hawkins

- [ ] *Everyone Here is Lying* by Shari Lapena

- [ ] *Brutes* by Dizz Tate

- [ ] *Sing, Unburied, Sing* by Jesmyn Ward

- [ ] *Americanah* by Chimamanda Ngozi Adichie

First Pages Checklist

01	My first pages offer access to the main point-of-view protagonist right away.	YES ☐	NO ☐
02	My first pages start in scene, with dialogue, action, or smaller-scale tension.	YES ☐	NO ☐
03	I do NOT start with level-ten conflict in my first pages, or there will be nowhere else to go from there.	YES ☐	NO ☐
04	I suggest or express my theme in a covert way.	YES ☐	NO ☐
05	My first pages open some loops and embed some hooks.	YES ☐	NO ☐

06   I've avoided using a prologue unless I absolutely need one.   YES ☐   NO ☐

07   I do NOT use a flashback or introduce backstory in the first scene. (Relevant backstory information can be woven in after the present action of the opening is established.)   YES ☐   NO ☐

Plot Checklist

01   I consider myself to be a:

     ☐ Plotter

     ☐ Pantser

02   I've made an outline for my plot structure (even if you're a pantser, sacrifice a few hours to try outlining, you'll learn a lot).   YES ☐   NO ☐

03   Have I given enough reason for the character to keep fighting when the going gets tough?   YES ☐   NO ☐

04   Have I made it easy to root for my protagonist, even if they fail, make mistakes, and/or forget their values?   YES ☐   NO ☐

05   All of my scenes and chapters matter—they introduce, reinforce, or change the reader's understanding of the protagonist, story, plot, relationships with other characters, or all of the above.   YES ☐   NO ☐

Plot Tentpole Questionnaire

In this section, you can play around with tentpole plot ideas. If you find you don't have much to say about any of these yet, that's useful data.

Inciting incident ideas:

_____

_____

_____

_____

Escalating obstacles ideas:

_____

_____

_____

_____

Midpoint ideas:

_____

_____

_____

_____

Dark night of the soul ideas (cont.):

_____

_____

Dark night of the soul ideas (cont.):

_____

_____

Synthesis climax ideas:

_____

_____

_____

_____

Ending ideas:

_____

_____

_____

_____

If you found some holes in your overall narrative, where might you want to brainstorm more about either the plot or the character development?

_____

_____

_____

_____

There are many plotting guides to choose from, like *Save the Cat Writes a Novel* by Jessica Brody, *Story Grid* by Shawn Coyne, and *The Story Solution* by Erik Edson. I've also developed a framework for my Story Mastermind small-group workshop. Download a free copy here: **bit.ly/novel-outline**

PART TWO

DEEP CHARACTER DEVELOPMENT

Backstory and Wound

It may surprise you that I'm starting Part 2 and our character focus by discussing backstory, which gets a bad rap in the writing world. I want to be clear, right away, that this is information you need to know for your own purposes as you're creating your protagonist. How much of it actually ends up on the page, when, and where, is another question entirely. This is the work of exposition, which must be undertaken lightly and gracefully. First, let's define the major topics at hand.

> **Backstory:** Every character has past events that have informed their identity leading up to the present. It's the writer's job to decide what these events entail, how detailed you get in rendering them, how much information is used, when, and how. To be effective, backstory must relate to the present and give readers added insight into character. As such, it should be used selectively and layered into a story gradually as the plot unfolds. Avoid large info-dumps of backstory, especially in the first few chapters, where dense information can easily crush your forward momentum. Backstory is crucial to know and think about because it offers a glimpse into a character's wound and misbelief. These elements will be embedded deeply within your protagonist and largely unconscious … at first.

Wound: This is a specific situation, event, or relationship in the past that's consciously or unconsciously keeping your character from realizing their full potential in the present. You can get specific about developing the circumstances that first plant the character's wound within their psyche. Even if a character believes they've healed—or compartmentalized—their trauma, their past will interfere with their ability to reach their objectives and remind them of their underlying need. Your primary question when developing the wound is: How does it help or hamper the character *now?*

Misbelief: This term can be used interchangeably with the idea of a character flaw. It's ideally connected to the wound, so that all of your character's "damage" is cohesive. Your protagonist might believe they are broken, not good enough, cowardly, powerless, or any other shameful deeply held idea. A compelling plot is designed to, in part, bring your protagonist to confront, change, or overcome their wound and misbelief. Ideally, that same plot will let them meet their deeper need, too.

A character's backstory matters to the present narrative, whether they like it or not. Protagonists should grapple with their past, wound, and misbelief, but their goal isn't necessarily to heal themselves forever. It's to integrate this early trauma so they're no longer held back (or held back as seriously) by what happened and who they became as a result. They aren't aiming for perfection, but to move forward with their heads held high and their needs nurtured at long last, which is no small task, either. In some instances, like the upmarket novel *Eleanor Oliphant Is Completely Fine* by Gail Honeyman, a piece of backstory is so incendiary that it's only revealed at the end. In these cases, curiosity hooks about what happened are everywhere. Other times, wounds and painful backstory events are merely alluded to, discussed, or thought about, but never explicitly narrated on the page. Finally, flashback can show crucial past events in scene.

Flashback: The narrative transitions to an encapsulated memory for a set period of time, whether one paragraph, ... (*cont.*)

Flashback (cont.): ... a scene, or several chapters. There's a beginning and end to this event, and the point of the flashback is to reveal important backstory. Flashbacks are useful for showing past events or characters who aren't available in the present, for whatever reason. This technique is effective when you have a fully realized moment which can be sustained, rather than a lot of quick, well, flashes. In essence, flashback is *how* you do it, and backstory is *what* you provide once there.

How and When to Use Backstory

The wound and backstory you explore will depend on the kind of project you're writing. In memoir, the past is very relevant and can take up the bulk of a manuscript. In romcom, we usually get a sense of romantic wounding in one or both characters' backstories and this interferes with their current ability to love or trust. Upmarket, women's, and literary fiction can also feature backstory elements, but these may or may not get a lot of attention in the present, unless there's a crucial thematic element of trauma or grief.

In mystery, thriller, suspense, and horror, various individual wounds tend to loom large in both the psychology of the victim(s) and the perpetrator of the danger. Backstory elements provide salient clues to the "whodunit" plot mechanic of a mystery story, or the "whydunit" dramatic question of a thriller. In fact, the past may be re-examined several times once new information emerges, as characters explore theories and clues, after twists, and when instances of misdirection pile up before the climactic reveal.

Writers often wonder how much backstory to develop for their main characters, and how much of it should end up on the page. The answer is: It varies. Especially if you're the flavor of writer who has journals and journals devoted to everything from your character's early life experiences to their favorite ice cream flavor. That's valid work, but some of it won't see the outside of those journals and you have to be okay with that. Too much information, especially to start, is, well, a non-starter. Audiences don't care about your character yet, so they certainly don't care about earlier versions of them. I admire that you've done this writing homework. This shows dedication. But a novel or memoir often rides the delicate balance between action and information. Why can't you simply explain everything you want readers to know?

Well, just like the spoonful of sugar helping the medicine go down, you need a delivery medium which won't make your target gag. Information, by itself, isn't built to engage. With a cold, hard start, it's unreasonable to expect your audience to suddenly plug into a list of biographical details about your character. Turn up your action, however, and the story gets rolling.

> **Balance of Action and Information:** Action moves quickly, while information tends to be dense and slow. Both are necessary for story (and to convey a compelling character on the page), but too much of either is a potential liability. Action tends to be "slippery" and doesn't engender much empathy, emotion, reflection, and understanding. Information is quite "sticky"—in that it provides context—but can also sink your pacing, which is the perceived speed at which your narrative moves. You should play around with the balance of these elements, adding small instances of context, backstory, and reaction to scenes, then interspersing high-stakes action with moments of reflection, memory, and strategy. Both action and information ebb and flow throughout a structure. If you find yourself indulging in too much data or interiority or hitting readers with scene after scene of conflict, introduce some action to break up heavy info-dumps or find places to fold in some information, respectively. How you'll strike this balance is depends on your writing style, category, and genre. It might also take some trial and error as you draft and revise.

In terms of introducing backstory and deploying it throughout the narrative, sometimes the most direct way is best. In other words, you'll do some telling, but the good kind. After all, how else is a reader supposed to know that characters practice mage magic on your planet, but the protagonist's powers failed to awaken? Or that a woman's bachelorette party was last Friday, but nobody showed up? Definitely don't show the bride pointing at a calendar with the date conspicuously circled, then crying and throwing away bags of unused party favors in a misguided attempt to "show, don't tell."

To "tell" is not a four-letter word in these instances, especially if the reader gets just enough data to understand what's going on. The ramifications of the backstory, whether traumatic or formative, will undergird the present-day character's behavior, wants, needs, worldview, and actions. Once readers know the history, they can speculate about its effects. A character wouldn't have meaningful present action without a sense of the future (in the form of objective, motivation, and need). Likewise, they would lack serious substance without the past and its attendant identity-shaping wounds and misbeliefs.

Once the present action is established and running smoothly, you can start thinking of how to layer in backstory. Less is more. We don't need the character's whole life story, Mom and Dad's history, and the family dog's provenance, unless this is an intergenerational saga. Generally, the earlier you are in your structure, the more often the backstory and wound are teased as a curiosity hook. Events are referenced but readers don't have context for them yet, which keeps audiences wondering: What happened? Why does it matter? Later in the story, more information is revealed and additional layers of meaning and understanding are added. In some genres, the whole puzzle doesn't snap together until the end. In putting together the following examples, I found that backstory generally runs the gamut from traumatic to formative. Sometimes it's both—the event was tough for the protagonist to overcome, but they have really grown as a result, which wouldn't have been possible without their wounding experience. Backstory can also be raw or mostly healed and can come from the recent or distant past.

Traumatic Backstory Text Analysis

Consider what the examples overleaf teach you about each character and how they are dealing (or not dealing) with traumatic events from their pasts?

Example 1:

He was a man of few words, preferring to keep his thoughts hidden, but that didn't bother me. He had always kept his distance, and his promises. (*Well, there was once but ... no.*) I forced the memory away.

Impressions of the POV character and backstory:

_____

_____

_____

How is interiority used?

_____

_____

_____

Example 2:

For me, gin is a necessary evil. It numbs the fear and pressure threatening to consume me every night. Mommy's voice echoes in my mind, and another small, timid one pleading for my help, over and over again, shattering me each time. Without my trusted medicine, I fear I, too, would shatter.

Impressions of the POV character and backstory:

_____

_____

_____

How is interiority used?

_____

_____

_____

The below character is looking at herself in the mirror after surviving a sexual assault.

Example 3:

I was consumed by my own ugliness. Every pore on my skin felt like a target luring him. His stare pinned me down, then came the touch. My body was numb, but my mind was acutely aware of every way I'd failed to measure up. In his eyes, I was nothing … and that's what was left when he was done with me.

Impressions of the POV character and backstory:

_____

_____

_____

How is interiority used?

_____

How is interiority used (cont.)?

_____

_____

Example 4:

His infidelity is no secret, and she has come to accept he will never be
faithful, so she remains in the picture, sweet and devoted as a nun. But he
insists there was only one other, a moment of weakness after the death of
their beloved baby. She remembers how lost she felt in her own grief,
questioning how she could go on. She couldn't help but wonder if this
tragedy was a form of cosmic karma, as her own birth stole her mother's
life. These dark thoughts consumed her, leaving teeth-marks even more
painful than his betrayal.

Impressions of the POV character and backstory:

_____

_____

_____

How is interiority used?

_____

_____

_____

Formative Backstory Text Analysis

The following examples demonstrate formative backstory for their respective characters. The events might still be painful but the degree to which the characters are affected—and what they do as a result of having lived through certain circumstances—might seem different.

> Our first character reads her old diary and is shocked to see how angry she used to be at her dad. With time, her feelings have mellowed.

Example 1:

My father had been a soldier, his mind and manners molded by the strict hierarchy which forged him. Maybe he was harsher than necessary, but I don't recall ever feeling this fever pitch of hatred. My memories have taken on the patina of nostalgia, burnishing his faults, smoothing over how I used to see him.

Impressions of the POV character and backstory:

_____

_____

_____

How is interiority used?

_____

_____

_____

> The next character offers a glimpse at her upbringing, suggesting why she might now be emotionally stunted.

Example 2:

My mother spoke in actions, not words. It was a skill I'd honed; it got me where I was. But is it an asset or a liability? I couldn't answer.

Impressions of the POV character and backstory:

_____

_____

_____

How is interiority used?

_____

_____

_____

This character realizes that love is essential for her survival (if she ever hopes to thrive). She then gathers the courage to say so to her father figure, only to be rebuffed.

Example 3:

I grit my teeth, struggling not to scream in his face because he simply doesn't understand. "I care about *your* opinion," I snapped. "You are all I have." But I knew he'd never say the words I longed to hear. He couldn't admit to loving me, and maybe he never did. And so, I made a new vow to stop caring altogether. My survival demanded it.

Impressions of the POV character and backstory:

_____

_____

_____

How is interiority used?

_____

_____

_____

> The below character is new to being wealthy and marvels at it.

Example 4:

As the words left her lips, she felt a pang of guilt. But it was true—
shopping was mind-numbingly dull. She glanced at her personal
shopping assistant, an unimaginable young thing who'd materialized
solely for her pleasure. Around them, ghosts of her past selves seemed to
swirl and ogle her glittering new outfits.

Impressions of the POV character and backstory:

_____

_____

_____

How is interiority used?

_____

_____

_____

This final character is thinking about not only her personal backstory but that of her indigenous ancestors, showing how cultural context can play into one's sense of self and history.

Example 5:

The resilience of her people depended on hiding in plain sight for lifetimes, masquerading as whatever fit the moment. But years of deception left their scars. She fights to hold onto the teachings of her ancestors, the value of collaboration and unity, but it's a constant battle.

Impressions of the POV character and backstory:

_____

_____

_____

How is interiority used?

_____

_____

_____

Backstory and Wound Checklist

Consider how backstory and wound factor into your work.

01   My protagonist has a character wound.   YES ☐   NO ☐

Write it here:

02   My protagonist has a misbelief.   YES ☐   NO ☐

Write it here:

03   If I'm employing flashbacks to communicate backstory, they're used sparingly.   YES ☐   NO ☐

My protagonist's backstory is:

04
☐ Traumatic

☐ Formative

☐ Both

Dig deeper into the above. How does your character's backstory affect them in the present? Way #1:

Way #2:

Way #3:

Brainstorm some potential flashbacks/memories your character might have here:

Sense of Self

Most humans have a deep and private identity, and so do our characters. How does a protagonist think to and about themselves? Their true opinions, insecurities, and reflections are often at odds with whatever the audience might see externally. A great way to demonstrate sense of self to readers is to have protagonists engage in self-assessment and self-inquiry, early and often, especially at consequential moments in the plot.

Audiences are going to form their own opinions of your character, and you absolutely want to encourage this process. Remember, a reader wants to be an active participant by thinking critically and generating their own impressions, which you will either confirm or subvert. However, this can only happen if you're aware of how your protagonist comes across in the first place. Interiority is especially suited to characters expressing how they feel about themselves, in their own words and thoughts.

This opens up a lot of interesting potential. Is your protagonist reliable, or perhaps unreliable, in their self-assessment? Too nice and maybe even delusional? Too harsh and perhaps suffering from their own misbelief or someone else's unfair expectations? Do they have low self-awareness or high? Low self-esteem or high? Do these attributes change over time? Their identity is also subject to internal tension, as we'll see later in this workbook.

More importantly, what kind of story does your character tell themselves about themselves? (In psychology, this is called the "internalized story of self.") Is the protagonist able to explore their own narrative identity and develop a nuanced self-understanding? Do they make meaning from experiences, then extrapolate and subsume those insights into their sense of being? Are they able to overcome their difficulties and achieve a redemptive growth arc? Or do they allow their moods and most recent successes and failures influence their self-perception. You don't have to answer all of these questions, but you should be aware that these options exist for characters, just as they do for human beings.

Personality types and styles are one jumping off-point into a character's sense of self. An example is the concept of fixed or growth mindsets, codified by Carol Dweck in *Mindset: The New Psychology of Success*. Her research centers on the idea that some people have a fixed mindset and tend to believe in set identity characteristics. This often correlates with lower self-awareness and passivity. Other people have a growth mindset, which opens them up to self-awareness, self- improvement, and proactive behavior. The former type of person focuses on all the reasons something is impossible, rather than finding opportunities to prevail. The latter type believes in the potential for self-driven change and growth.

The character's relationship to their inner self guides the reader's relationship to character. One of the benefits of being human is that we have the capacity for self-awareness—though not everyone uses theirs! As such, most sentient beings have longstanding and nuanced ideas who they are. These notions guide their actions and thoughts, and can also be flexible as protagonists change and grow (or, less often, regress). Sense of self can be determined by others (for the least aware and evolved characters), are created by the self but flexible to outside influence, or can be internally generated and fairly consistent.

More Sense of Self Considerations

- A character with a fragile sense of self might not be able to come to their own conclusions, instead wondering: What will others think?

- Consider "code-switching," which means characters act differently in specific situations and with various groups of people. Does your character display certain behaviors with family that they'd never dare show their friends? In a professional setting or while goofing off? How does this factor into their identity? How do they feel about it?
- Going from feeling defined by others to standing by your own sense of self is actually a huge leap. This kind of growth arc is very common in middle grade, young adult, memoir, and some women's and upmarket fiction, where more profound transformation is often expected.
- A protagonist's role within their larger interpersonal framework is an interesting identity layer. Consider birth order and sibling rivalry. Studies have found differences between only children and those with siblings; first children, middle children, and younger children; and in children from big families and small ones. How might various family roles inform your character's identity?
- Moral code. Values. Integrity. These are all things to consider as you build out who your protagonist is at their deepest core.
- Intentional actions reflect on the self. Unintentional actions, failed attempts, and mistakes do, too. Identity can be shaped by both presence and absence—what did happen, and what didn't.
- Characters often present with a dreary sense of self and feel damaged when they succumb to their wounds or act outside of their values.
- It's up to you to decide whether your struggling characters will redeem themselves with morally solid choices. Antihero protagonists can still engage readers despite their behavior, but fostering this connection may be tougher.
- Not all plot conflicts are external. Plenty of characters put internal obstacles in their own way, consciously or not, due to fear, vulnerability, or self-defeating tendencies. Sometimes this is understandable and warranted, but it's detrimental all the same.
- There's an old adage: "Wherever you go, there you are." Some characters, especially those with low self-esteem, will pursue the objective of leaving their "old self" or "old life" behind. This goal tends to be fueled by an early-story misbelief, as meaningful transformation is not as easy as a location change.

- Some writers like to be very specific about a character's appearance, while others take a lighter approach and let readers mentally fill in the blanks. At some point, though, no matter your preference, you will have to provide a physical description of your protagonist, so try to avoid well-known contrivances. The most common cliché is a character looking in the mirror and relaying what they see. But what they notice about themselves—and how they subsume it—makes such self-description in interiority feel fresh. Also note that appearance information is often more awkward to provide in first person POV than in third. In fact, "third-person-style" self-description in first person can be a huge voice issue. Consider this: "I swept my bangs aside with my left hand, looking for all the world like the light in my eyes had gone out." This sounds like something a narrator might say about a character, but I'm hard-pressed to imagine someone saying this about themselves. How often do we think about the basic stats of our appearance, after all? It's too overly self-conscious. If you're guilty of this in your first-person writing, decide how you want to tackle the question of describing the character's external actions and qualities, and whether your efforts sound organic. You might also want to do less with descriptions of individual physical actions, or "play-by-play choreography." In the above example, do we really need to know which hand was used to touch the bangs? No. These details are often superficial and less interesting than what interiority can convey. Keep them to a minimum.

Low Sense of Self Text Analysis

The following characters have low self-awareness, self-esteem, or define their sense of self from what they believe others think of them.

> The below character is giving out drugs at a club to try and make friends, but isn't too optimistic about his odds.

Example 1:

"Wanna party?" He flashed the pills in his palm, knowing deep down that they, like countless others, would forget him by the end of the night.

Impressions of the character:

_____

_____

_____

How is interiority used?

_____

_____

_____

What's it like to be him?

_____

_____

_____

The character below has accidentally revealed a family secret, putting her sister's livelihood in danger in a dystopian society.

Example 2:

My actions today caused immeasurable damage to those dearest to me. I'm tempted to crawl home, to face the consequences. Yet here I sit, a coward, hidden in the shadows and roiling in darkness. *Perhaps pain is my purpose. If only everyone would forget me, they'd be better off.*

Impressions of the character:

_____

_____

_____

How is interiority used?

_____

_____

_____

What's it like to be her?

_____

_____

_____

Our next character wants to give up on her life and is wishing her partner would help her destroy herself (figuratively).

Example 3:

I could sense the bile rising in my throat, a sickening concoction of food and my own organs. I wanted to expel it all, rid myself of this skin, this body. Maybe if he stepped on my heart, squeezed the life out of it, I could finally be free.

Impressions of the character:

_____

_____

Impressions of the character (cont.):

_____

How is interiority used?

_____

_____

_____

What's it like to be her?

_____

_____

_____

The next character is so obsessed with authorial success that he plagiarizes a friend's manuscript and justifies his actions.

Example 4:

Envy, for writers, is a gnawing sense of terror, a sharp spike in my heart rate at every mention of his success on social media. The constant comparisons and self-doubt consume me, the relentless knowledge that I will never measure up. Even the news of his latest six-figure first-look streaming deal sends me spiraling into distraction and self-loathing for days, unable to shift the shame and jealousy whenever I pass a window with his books prominently displayed.

Impressions of the character:

_____

_____

Impressions of the character (cont.):

_____

How is interiority used?

_____

_____

_____

What's it like to be him?

_____

_____

_____

> The next character is thinking of how she might fit in with some friends
> who she believes are above her.

Example 5:

She lacked Cassie's sharp edges, or Scott's brazen humor. But she could
still transform into someone else entirely, perhaps even someone Keith
would notice. The mere thought sent goosebumps rising on her bare skin
beneath the delicate fabric of her new dress.

Impressions of the character:

_____

_____

_____

How is interiority used?

_____

_____

_____

What's it like to be her?

_____

_____

_____

The following character grapples with aging and finds out her old self-deprecating humor no longer works.

Example 6:
"You won't remember me," she joked, regretting the overture immediately. In her youth, she'd wielded that line like a precise weapon. As if she could ever be forgettable. But now her looks didn't merit a second glance. Nobody *actually* remembered her.

Impressions of the character:

_____

_____

_____

How is interiority used?

_____

_____

How is interiority used (cont.)?

_____

What's it like to be her?

_____

_____

_____

Growing Sense of Self Text Analysis

In the following examples, the characters are either normally more self-aware or they're developing in their sense of self.

> This character has lived under her mother's thumb for her entire life and is struggling to differentiate herself from her mother's expectations.

Example 1:

Each shopping trip is a battle. I force myself to play the game, but my decision-making muscles have shriveled from lack of use. I try to imagine myself in different outfits or jewelry, but I just see Mom's vision of me. Rather than stare right at it, I close my eyes and then I can pretend again.

Impressions of the character:

_____

_____

_____

How is interiority used?

_____

_____

_____

What's it like to be her?

_____

_____

The following twentysomething resents having to pretend to be okay.

Example 2:

Do people ever truly feel the weight of my emotional armor? Or do they only see the polished surface I've carefully crafted to hide the vulnerable parts within? They're unaware of the red, raw marks left on my shoulders by this weight. It's as if they refuse to acknowledge my potential, seeing only their expectations.

Impressions of the character:

_____

_____

_____

How is interiority used?

_____

_____

_____

What's it like to be him?

_____

_____

_____

The next character is struggling with her own problems and stands up to her parent, who is attempting to dump issues on her.

Example 3:
"You need therapy," I say, not meaning to sound callous. She desperately needs someone to confide in, and with my own stuff going on, I'm woefully unequipped to help.

Impressions of the character:

_____

_____

_____

How is interiority used?

_____

_____

_____

What's it like to be her?

_____

_____

The last character in this section finally admits to having suffered a
traumatic assault, and waits for the worst-case scenario to happen.

Example 4:
I summoned the courage to speak the words out loud. As they hung in the air, I waited for catastrophe. Yet the Earth held steady beneath my feet. Everything was just as it was before. Except for me. I was changed.

Impressions of the character:

_____

_____

_____

How is interiority used?

_____

_____

_____

What's it like to be her?

_____

_____

_____

High Sense of Self Text Analysis

The below characters have high self-awareness and a clear sense of identity.

Our first character is comparing his younger self to his current middle-aged incarnation.

Example 1:

Did he despise the arrogant young man he used to be? That self-absorbed asshole? Or did he loathe the older man he'd become, seemingly overnight? In a way, he detested both. His aged self had unwittingly betrayed his young self. This shell of a man now had a mortgage, a 401(k), a fancy job requiring suits and ties, a marriage, a child. All things his younger self would have scoffed at. He was no longer true to his ideals. He clipped coupons and woke up early. And worst of all, he cringed catching a glimpse of his tattoo. How could these two vastly different versions of himself coexist?

Impressions of the character:

_____

_____

_____

How is interiority used?

_____

_____

_____

What's it like to be him?

_____

_____

The next character is in a relationship for money and reflects on her choice.

Example 2:

That's what you pay me for, she thought but didn't say. It was easier to stay silent. She cared for him, in a way. So it wasn't an epic love story. Wasn't companionship enough? Did every relationship need to be defined by passion? Maybe true love was overrated. She figured, deep down, she could continue like this for years.

Impressions of the character:

_____

_____

_____

How is interiority used?

_____

_____

_____

What's it like to be her?

_____

_____

_____

The next character, Annie, disagrees with her mother's illegal business, where she scams her friends. Though she gets flack for it, Annie holds her head held high when challenged.

Example 3:

The boundary between exploitation and kindness was lost on Momma. No matter how hot Momma's anger burned, Annie refused to lie in the Lord's name. "Ungrateful child," Momma spat, "foolish child. You'll come to nothing." But Annie stood her ground, even when it would've been easier to play the game. "Let me come to nothing, at least I won't have to explain to Jesus why I lied to all my friends."

Impressions of the character:

_____

_____

_____

How is interiority used?

_____

_____

_____

What's it like to be her?

_____

_____

_____

The following character breaks her time period's gender norms by doing a traditionally male job.

Example 4:

I relished the sensation of their gazes upon me, assessing my value. And yet, I stood tall, confident in my own worth.

Impressions of the character:

_____

_____

_____

How is interiority used?

_____

_____

_____

What's it like to be her?

_____

_____

_____

Sense of Self Questionnaire

You don't have to answer all of these questions, but you should be aware of your character identity options.

01   Is your protagonist reliable in their self-assessment?

YES ☐   NO ☐

02 Do they have low self-awareness or high? HI ☐ LO ☐

03 Do they have low self-esteem or high? HI ☐ LO ☐

04 Do these attributes change over time? YES ☐ NO ☐

05 What's their mindset type?

☐ **Fixed:** Tends to believe that identity characteristics are set. This often correlates with lower self-awareness and passivity.

☐ **Growth:** Open to self-awareness, self-improvement, and proactive behavior.

06 What kind of story does your character tell themselves *about* themselves and who they are?

Write it here:

07 Is the protagonist able to explore their own identity and develop a nuanced self-understanding? YES ☐ NO ☐

08 Do they make meaning from experiences then extrapolate and subsume those insights into their sense of self? YES ☐ NO ☐

09 Are they able to overcome their difficulties and achieve a redemptive arc (as opposed to allowing their moods and most recent successes and failures to influence their self-perception)?

YES ☐   NO ☐

Exploring Sense of Self

Start brainstorming your protagonist's deep self.

The character's impressions of their own identity:

How might you use interiority to convey this? Examples:

Objective and Motivation

Simply put, readers care about characters who care about something. The idea of striving toward an outcome, big or small, is universally relatable. A protagonist's objective matters and tends to make them proactive, to boot. The origin of a compelling desire is often tied to a character's backstory, whether they're aware of it or not. An objective, and the driving logic behind it, can also change and deepen over the course of a story.

> **Objective:** What a character wants. This can be superficial (generally seen toward the beginning of a story) or substantial (generally seen as the character's sense of self evolves). The want can be internal or external, or both.

> **Motivation:** The reason a character wants what they do. This logic can be conscious or unconscious. Motivations can also transition as characters grow, change, or become more self-aware. Objective and motivation are usually coupled together, though the same motivation can drive multiple objectives.

The concepts of objective and motivation will help readers understand what a character is doing, why, and how these elements circle back to their sense of self. If a reader understands the reason a protagonist does or says something, or acts a certain way in a certain context, they will be more compelled. Interiority is fantastic at conveying these layers. Objective and motivation also help clarify a character's expectations when they go into a scene, and suggest what they imagine (or fear) will happen during and after. By following along with what a protagonist wants and knowing why they want it, readers will also be able to extrapolate how the outcome of each attempt to triumph might affect the character and their trajectory. This brings me to a key point: Readers must often infer objective and, especially, motivation from interiority. Since we're now drilling into deeper layers of protagonist development, we aren't going to find too many overt statements which blatantly explain these concepts. This is where your audience will really start doing their detective work—and it's an opportunity to keep enticing them with your masterful use of interiority.

Sometimes objectives that a character actively pursues are called "approach," and those they avoid in order to stave off consequences are called "avoidance." Imagine running toward something versus running away. We can also call them "positive" and "negative" objectives. I strongly suggest you choose to focus on building positive approach objectives rather than giving protagonists negative avoidance ones. Characters who pursue something—rather than trying to hide from harm—tend to read as much more proactive and heroic.

Now that theme, plot, character background, and selfhood have been established, it's time to kick everything into motion. The most powerful tools for putting rocket boosters on a story, especially in the beginning, are character objective and motivation.

More Objective and Motivation Considerations

Stay active in your development of a character's objective and motivation. Every time an objective or motivation shifts, track it. Put some interiority on the page about the change of heart. This is a turning point, which we'll discuss in a bit. Give the reader enough data to understand the character's logic. Objective and motivation can change independently of one another or shift together. They can morph as a result of small moments and big ones. These transitions can come quickly or gradually. They can connect to plot tentpoles or be spread over the course of an entire story, similar to a character arc. In the beginning of your story, you should establish objective and motivation as early as is natural. Initial character drivers are likely to be superficial, and that's okay. As long as readers get a sense that your character is actively pursuing something, ideally something relevant to the larger plot, you are doing your job and offering audiences a sense of immediate context and conflict. Have the protagonist look to the future and share their dreams or expectations.

In psychology, we find the idea of extrinsic and intrinsic motivations. The former term refers to people and characters who choose to do something because they perceive it will have external value (climbing the career ladder, donating to charity with the goal of getting acclaim, etc.). The latter refers to activities that people and characters choose to do because they consider them internally motivating, interesting, or fulfilling. Here, we can see the distinction between an external objective and a deeper need.

Remember to also track the character's experience as they give up certain objectives or outgrow them. How do they talk to themselves about what they wanted once upon a time and didn't get, or are actively abandoning? What are some selfish or superficial emotions this might stir up? Many layers of thoughts, feelings, reactions, expectations, and inner struggles can become involved here.

Lessons from the Theatre

Konstantin Stanislavsky, a famous Russian director whose methods are still taught today, has an important thought experiment for actors—the "seven questions." These are also useful for writers, especially when it comes to crafting character.

Here are the five most relevant questions (out of the seven):

1. Who am I?
2. What do I want?
3. Why do I want it?
4. How will I get what I want?
5. What must I overcome to get what I want?

As you can see, want features heavily in Stanislavsky's idea of character development. Now let's apply this line of inquiry to *your* protagonist.

The Five Questions

Take a stab at these as your character ... or yourself, if you're feeling existential!

Who am I?

What do I want?

Why do I want it?

How will I get what I want?

What must I overcome to get what I want?

Extrinsic Objective Text Analysis

Let's begin with examples of characters with extrinsic objectives ... though some of these instances suggest deeper wants and needs.

> The below character's son is struggling in school. When the head of the PTA asks her to compromise her professional values and give her special treatment, she vacillates.

Example 1:

She considered the weight of having Dolores owe her a favor. The thought of Jake's potential outbursts souring his reputation at school filled her with anxiety. Public schools had resources and support for behavioral issues, but private schools were less forgiving. They could simply expel students without question, leaving her—and Jake, of course—to face the daunting task of starting over again and again. But if she had Dolores on her side? The queen of the Lakeside PTA? The school's biggest fundraiser? There was safety in that idea.

What is the objective?

_____

_____

_____

What is the motivation?

_____

_____

_____

What might be underneath both the objective and motivation?

_____

_____

_____

> The next character has immigrated to a new country and imagines what it
> might feel like to fit in there.

> ## Example 2:
>
> She relished the illusion, above all else, that in this realm of privileged
> comfort, she could masquerade as anyone, a chosen member of a secret
> club, adorned with impenetrable confidence.

What is the objective?

_____

_____

_____

What is the motivation?

_____

_____

_____

What might be underneath both the objective and motivation?

_____

_____

_____

The following character believes a love match will change her life.

Example 3:

Fortune smiled upon me at just the right moment. Tonight, I would finally be made whole. The anticipation clawed at my insides, a sweet pain not even cold gin could numb. I knew I had to endure it until our fateful meeting. A few more hours, and I would be forever altered by his touch. I was ready to be molded into a new likeness, made in his image, my past erased.

What is the objective?

_____

_____

_____

What is the motivation?

_____

_____

_____

What might be underneath both the objective and motivation?

_____

_____

_____

The next character is a workaholic who's trying to avoid thinking about a recent upsetting event.

Example 4:

The thought of staying home and dwelling on it made my skin crawl. My boss had to let me work, even if it meant me begging.

What is the objective?

_____

_____

_____

What is the motivation?

_____

_____

_____

What might be underneath both the objective and motivation?

_____

_____

_____

The next character has the potential to ruin his co-worker's career after discovering something secret about her. Here's his thought process.

Example 5:

He knew he should reveal himself to her, but the thought of losing his strategic upper hand made him hesitate. *This is my defining moment,* he thought, *the line between success and failure.* He weighed his options. Share his true identity and risk ruining everything? Or keep playing the game for just a little longer?

What is the objective?

_____

_____

_____

What is the motivation?

_____

_____

_____

What might be underneath both the objective and motivation?

_____

_____

_____

Intrinsic Objective Text Analysis

Now let's do a bit more digging into some internally focused objectives.

The first character in this section has run away to "work on a book" but admits she wasn't exactly honest about her intentions. Meanwhile, she feels responsible for her father's situation and subsumes a negative sense of self.

Example 1:

This Sheraton was supposed to be my creative sanctuary for the next seven days. Yet deep down, I know that no matter where I go, I cannot escape the truth; as my father's life falls apart, I can't see beyond the all-consuming echo chamber of my own skull.

What is the objective?

_____

_____

_____

What is the motivation?

_____

_____

_____

What might be underneath both the objective and motivation?

_____

_____

_____

> The next character has avoided entering a contest for her hobby, only to realize what she'd missed.

Example 2:

For three long years, she almost dared to enter, but self-doubt always held her back. Even last year, she filled out the forms, only to let fear win at the last moment. But now, standing here among her peers, she regrets not coming sooner. A fierce desire swells within her. She doesn't just want to place—she wants victory with every fiber of her being.

What is the objective?

_____

What is the objective (cont.)?

_____

_____

What is the motivation?

_____

_____

What might be underneath both the objective and motivation?

_____

_____

_____

This character has been struggling with disordered eating.

Example 3:

She can sense it, when the insatiable part of her mind awakens. It's like a switch flipping on, unleashing a primal hunger which devours her every trace of self-control. We all have our own inner monsters. Some crave carnal pleasure, others thirst for power, and some chase a high. And her? After years of barely surviving on scraps—her beast demands to be fed.

What is the objective?

_____

_____

What is the objective (cont.)?

_____

What is the motivation?

_____

_____

What might be underneath both the objective and motivation?

_____

_____

_____

This protagonist is dissatisfied with her mother-daughter relationship.

Example 4:

My longing consumed me. But my actual mother, who birthed and raised me, wouldn't do. No, my soul ached for the fictional embodiment of a nurturing, loving mama. This fantasy was born from years of emptiness, withholding. But I couldn't even conjure her, I didn't have the imagination to fathom such a woman.

What is the objective?

_____

_____

_____

What is the motivation?

_____

_____

_____

What might be underneath both the objective and motivation?

_____

_____

_____

> The last character in this section is thinking of what she wants from the
> man who assaulted her.

Example 5:

The thought of revenge crosses my mind, but it quickly dissipates. I don't crave retribution, only a simple apology. But what would he apologize for? For taking off my clothes without a single word? For not giving me the chance to protest? Yet, how can I blame him when I couldn't even find the words to stop him?

He should have known better. But deep down, I don't want him to feel sorry because he sees me as pathetic. I want him to sincerely regret his actions because he truly cares about me. A futile wish, perhaps, but one that still lingers in my heart.

What is the objective?

_____

_____

_____

What is the motivation?

_____

_____

_____

What might be underneath both the objective and motivation?

_____

_____

_____

Objective and Motivation Questionnaire

Make sure you're on the right track with your project.

01   Is your character's objective explained by a motivation?   YES ☐   NO ☐

02   Does the initial objective mature or change?   YES ☐   NO ☐

03   Does the motivation or objective tie into their backstory?   YES ☐   NO ☐

04   Are they able to be proactive in pursuing their objective?   YES ☐   NO ☐

05   What's their type of objective?

☐ Intrinsic   ☐ Both

☐ Extrinsic

06

Is their objective actually attainable, even if it's difficult or unlikely?

YES ☐ **NO** ☐

How does their objective transition or transform over time?

What do they pursue after the midpoint?

How has the objective changed by the end of the story?

How does the character talk to themselves about their objective as it changes?

If the character fails to attain their objective, how do they talk to themselves about this failure?

How do they subsume or reframe whatever happens regarding their objective, if they don't get it?

Need

You'll have to excuse me for being cheeky, but a character's need is an expression of what they ... need. It's as simple and as complex as that, since a protagonist's need can be straightforward or anything but. Of course, we all have basic needs—air, shelter, food, water. But these are typically not the kinds of needs that characters concern themselves with, except in scenes of acute danger, when all other problems and internal tensions fall away. Once a person or character's physical needs are taken care of, they become more concerned with striving for self-actualization.

This goes back to the idea of a proactive protagonist, one who has an internal locus of control, is intrinsically motivated, and actively drives their destiny. Needs that serve character creation and growth are emotional in nature and get to the very marrow of a protagonist's identity, maturation, and sense of achievement and proactivity over the course of the story.

> **Need:** While the objective is what the character might want, the need is what they should pursue to become complete. It often emerges once writers and readers understand the protagonist's identity-specific desire, which is created by their backstory and wound. Need is much more vulnerable than objective, and more important.

For a character to express a need, they must have self-awareness and do self-inquiry. For a reader to infer a need, they will have to do extrapolation and bring their sense of empathy to the page. That's why need is so crucial to character development, and such a juicy way to use interiority. Once you hit upon a compelling character need and plant it at the core of your protagonist, you will motivate readers to engage on the most intimate level yet.

Secrets are powerful forces in storytelling, creating curiosity hooks, conflict, and intrigue. A need is like a secret that your characters keep under heavy lock and key, sometimes even from themselves. Need-generating wounds often start out as painful or shameful events. You can use secrets to create plot tension, and you can use needs as wellsprings of character inner tension.

Objective and motivation might initially spring your character into action, but need is what keeps them going through the toughest and most discouraging parts of the plot, especially once they come to realize what's really happening below the surface.

The phrase "reading into" perfectly encapsulates an audience's role, and this is especially relevant to need. By interpreting, they are "reading into" the author's intentions and the character's interiority-based self-revelations. From what might seem like a superficial statement, at first blush, readers can glean a lot of insight into the protagonist. Need demands that audiences put on their thinking caps and dive right in, as these pearls must be retrieved from the depths.

Backstory, flashback, and wound are intimately tied to a character's need. If the wound is an absence of love in childhood, the character might crave love and chase it for the first half of the story. Unfortunately, they could also unknowingly recreate false beliefs and flawed ideas about love. By trying to correct for a distant parent who withheld affection, they might date a very sweet partner who's always around. Of course, this could prove to be the wrong approach and leave the character feeling smothered. They'll then have to interrogate their notion of love, which might involve self-inquiry and, ideally, healing.

Need Patterns

Character and human desires tend to define who we are on the most profound levels. If you think about needs in terms of conscious and unconscious, external and internal, you might start to notice what I like to call "want versus need," which is what someone wishes was true about themselves, but isn't. For example, they want to be easygoing, but are easily ruffled. This creates a problem only when they convince themselves that it's "better" to be easygoing. This misbelief can come from other characters judging them, or their subsumation of cultural and social messaging.

A character arriving at this worldview is influenced by the kinds of people and ideas they're surrounding themselves with. If they listen to a lot of "hustle culture" podcasts, they might start to believe that rest and play are slothful and frivolous. On the other hand, they could see "the cult of busyness" as driving a burnout epidemic. If a protagonist perceives part of their personality as a flaw and extrapolates the idea that something's "wrong" with them, they might attempt to "fix" the attribute in question. They might also convince themselves that other people don't struggle with the same issue, or struggle *as much*. This is often a misbelief.

What the protagonist wants is to be "normal," or more socially acceptable, and this fights their profound need to accept themselves or lean into their natural traits. You might find a character whose objective and motivation do a big 180 when they switch to being driven by their need because they realize their goal was founded on false principles to begin with.

Denial of one's needs—which requires conscious awareness of the need, then a rejection of it—is often seen in romcom, romance, and women's fiction. These are character-driven categories and genres where protagonists have to overcome certain hurdles within themselves in order to reach their full potential and a sense of present happiness, outside of close relationships and within them. To this end, needs don't always inspire action, especially if a character becomes aware of their need before they're fully capable of meeting it or addressing their wound. (We'll meet some internally conflicted example characters and see them run the other way until they're more prepared to tackle the real nature of their problems later.)

Needs, like objectives, often exist within a larger context rather than in isolation. A protagonist's growth journey typically involves letting go of their requirements for others (acceptance, validation, etc.) and working to be their own hero. After all, people and characters can only control themselves (and not always!), and the more they rely on other people for fulfillment, the more likely they are to be disappointed. Not because other people will always let us down (this sounds like a worldview statement, which we'll also learn about in a moment), but because our deepest necessities are best met internally.

Some characters, of course, are broken by their wounds and past or current experiences. They don't hold out much hope for realizing their own needs, let alone getting them met. I'll begin our text analysis by featuring some broken people to showcase how characters act out as a result of unaddressed desires. In almost all cases, the real issue is a lack of self-worth and self-love. True self-actualization is rare and difficult to do, but it's also the most sacred gift most characters (and people) can give themselves.

Buried Need Text Analysis

The following protagonists are not yet aware of—or active in pursuing—their needs, so we have to dig.

This fantasy character feels the spirits of the woods, which she believes in, have turned their backs on her. Her village wants her to be "normal," and she grapples with pressure from all sides.

Example 1:

The night dragged on, and a tiny part of her had clung to the possibility of salvation in the woods. She had dared to dream of the fiery phoenix, enchanted steed, or raven who practiced sorcery, that one or the other would save her. What a fool child, to believe in fantasies. The winter forest showed no mercy for humans—its spirits slumbered during this frigid season, and there was no such thing as a conjurer-raven, anyway.

What does the character say or suggest they need?

_____

_____

_____

Why might this need exist?

_____

_____

_____

What might actually fill this need?

_____

_____

_____

This young character wishes to escape his family.

Example 2:

I can hear the distant chirping of birds overhead. They're winging north, leaving this place behind, soaring high into the endless blue. I wish to join them but all I feel is a weight in my stomach, heavy and unshakeable, like the striking force at the end of a hammer.

What does the character say or suggest they need?

_____

_____

_____

Why might this need exist?

_____

_____

_____

What might actually fill this need?

_____

_____

_____

> The following character (mistakenly) believes her "sugar daddy" has
> decided to settle down with her.

Example 3:

Others had come before her, drifting in with their weekend bags and
poised, tentative bodies. They roamed the kitchen in the morning, sipping
coffee brewed by someone else. Fragile girls in flimsy camisoles, snacking
on yogurt in the light of an open fridge. But she'd endured, transcending
into a realm of permanence. Those girls became ghosts while she
remained, solid. Her clothes hung in the closet, marking her presence for
the summer, at least. She was invulnerable, no longer at risk of fading
away.

What does the character say or suggest they need?

_____

_____

_____

Why might this need exist?

_____

_____

_____

What might actually fill this need?

_____

_____

_____

My Take: This example was tricky! Here, the character thinks about what makes her different from the "others." She claims she's "[transcended] into a realm of permanence." This is a misbelief. She's as disposable as the rest, convincing herself she's "no longer at risk of fading away." What she claims to already have (security, lack of vulnerability) is what she needs.

Up next is a hardened character in a dangerous profession, observing her surroundings.

Example 4:

After living a life of constant threat, I find the world is no longer a carefree place, but a battlefield where I must always be on guard. Walking into a restaurant, I'm calculating the potential risks. Once you've witnessed the horrors lurking around every corner, there is no turning back. You can't _un_learn it. Even if you want to.

What does the character say or suggest they need?

_____

_____

What does the character say or suggest they need (cont.)?

_____

Why might this need exist?

_____

_____

_____

What might actually fill this need?

_____

_____

_____

Aware Need Text Analysis

The following characters are more able to acknowledge their needs, though they might still face obstacles to actively pursing them.

> The following character is traumatized after her baby is kidnapped.

Example 1:

I was consumed by a mad desire to stay awake, just in case he returned. My sweet baby had been snatched from the room next to mine, and I had slept through it all. How could I call myself a mother? So each night, I remained vigilant, imagining I'd turn the corner and find him in his room, smiling from his crib as if nothing had happened.

What does the character say or suggest they need?

_____

What does the character say or suggest they need (cont.)?

_____

_____

Why might this need exist?

_____

_____

_____

What might actually fill this need?

_____

_____

_____

This character is examining a picture of herself taken before a tragedy.

Example 2:

I almost don't recognize her, that ungainly, almost-ugly-almost-beautiful girl. How I yearn to start anew, to remember what it feels like to wear her skin. I study her eyes intently, as if they hold the map back to myself. The goal was to heal, but that seems impossible. I can't even fathom recovering some whisper of okay.

What does the character say or suggest they need?

_____

_____

_____

Why might this need exist?

_____

_____

_____

What might actually fill this need?

_____

_____

_____

The following tween character is taken to a nutritionist by her mother.

Example 3:

Mother prodded me toward the nutritionist, who appraised me with sharp eyes and a quick nod of approval. "You have it easy," she said, flashing her teeth. But beneath my relief, a tiny seed of distress sprouted unexpectedly. A small part of me had hoped to hear I was fine just the way I was, and that the real journey was learning to accept myself. Yet here I stood, confronted with a verdict that my body needed to change, whether I wanted it to or not.

What does the character say or suggest they need?

_____

_____

_____

Why might this need exist?

_____

Why might this need exist (cont.)?

_____

_____

What might actually fill this need?

_____

_____

> The next character is considering a stranger's potential racial identity as a
> clue to whether he might be a friend or a foe.

Example 4:

With his unnaturally wide grin, he seems familiar to Lux at first. As he
speaks, she's entranced by his smooth words, his charm. He looks a bit
like her a bit—maybe he's one of hers—but he could also look like
anyone. It suddenly dawns on her that this must've been the same tactic
used by colonizers who smiled falsely while ripping away what was once
shared by all. His ambiguous looks allow him to blend in anywhere, to
infiltrate with ease. Now Lux seethes at this man, who plays at being
everything and nothing at the same time.

What does the character say or suggest they need?

_____

_____

Why might this need exist?

_____

Why might this need exist (cont.)?

_____

_____

What might actually fill this need?

_____

_____

_____

Explicit Need Text Analysis

The following characters are both aware of their needs and doing something to pursue them.

Our first character is on vacation but hating it because of the company.

Example 1:

With a tilt of her head, she gazes upwards at the looming clouds, already anticipating another night locked in these four walls, with these terrible people. But she can't contain it any longer. She opens her mouth wide and unleashes a guttural scream towards the unforgiving sky, feeling the strain in her throat but also the sweet release of pent-up frustration.

What does the character say or suggest they need?

_____

_____

_____

Why might this need exist?

_____

_____

_____

What might actually fill this need?

_____

_____

_____

This character is running through a terrifying fantasy world.

Example 2:

I'll die here. The darkness of the tombs encroached upon her, impenetrable. She begged the heavens, or anyone who had any jurisdiction in this wretched place. *I'll never dabble in magic again, I'll take a husband—any husband. My freedom for my life.*

What does the character say or suggest they need?

_____

_____

_____

Why might this need exist?

_____

_____

_____

What might actually fill this need?

_____

_____

_____

This fantasy character longs to be "normal" (whatever that means), but she can't be. She is a mortal forced to live in the fairy realm and will never truly know what it's like to fit in anywhere. This might seem like a dream come true to some, but she knows better.

Example 3:

I can't help but wonder about the life I could have had, free from the burdens of magic. A normal existence, a mundane school, a head full of ordinary things. With alive parents and without this terrible anger. But as I let myself imagine, panic grips me. I cannot have it and I do not want it. I will always be here, paying for my sins.

What does the character say or suggest they need?

_____

_____

_____

Why might this need exist?

_____

_____

_____

What might actually fill this need?

_____

This character is expected to maintain and even expand the family's legacy but ... he doesn't wanna.

Example 4:

Born into the shadow of privilege, he was bound by expectation. He had to uphold his family's reputation. But in his heart, all he yearned for was to vanish, to shed his lineage. His father had plenty of other sons. What could he be if freed from the constraints of his name?

What does the character say or suggest they need?

Why might this need exist?

What might actually fill this need?

Crafting Layered Need

Here's how we can dig deep to unearth a compelling need.

If the wound is an absence of love in childhood:

> The character might crave love and chase it for the first half of the story. Unfortunately, they could also unknowingly recreate false beliefs and flawed ideas about love.

By trying to correct for a distant parent who withheld affection ...

> They might date a doting partner.

Of course, this could prove to be the wrong approach and leave the character feeling smothered.

> They'll then have to interrogate their notion of love, which might involve self-inquiry and, ideally, healing. It's not until the protagonist tries to "solve the problem the wrong way" first that they might realize the deeper ramifications of what's driving their need.

This character could come to understand their wound's origin—it wasn't Mom and Dad's distance, but their *conditional* love. Growing up, the protagonist had to perfectly anticipate and execute on expectations, or the parents would withhold affection and approval.

> The objective might be "love," but the need might be something more specific: **unconditional love**. And beneath that: **self-love**.

Exploring Need

What does your character say or suggest they need?

What might actually fill this need?

How does their awareness of need change around the midpoint?

What actions do they take to pursue their need?

How does their relationship to their need change during the crisis, dark night of the soul, or climax?

Do they get their need met (or set themselves up to have it met in the future) by the end?

What would it feel like to have this need met, after all? What would it mean to them?

Inner Struggle

Every character wrestles with something internally. In Lisa Cron's *Story Genius*, she calls inner struggle a story's "third rail" because it powers everything else your protagonist goes through. What is your character's big internal turmoil? How you present it matters, too, as straightforward explanation probably isn't the best strategy. Readers want to see the protagonist actually wrestling with an idea. This is what interiority was made for, so take it out for a spin.

You will absolutely want to introduce an element of your character's inner struggle in the first chapter of your novel or memoir, if you can. This is easy to do, since the protagonist is usually spinning their wheels in their "normal" before the inciting incident, superficially presenting as okay but somehow dissatisfied. (This is what can set them up to go on a journey of internal and, often, external transformation to begin with.) The flavor of this inner conflict should align with the backstory, wound, objective, and need, but you have many options to choose from, as you'll see in the following examples. You'll want to limit your character's expression of inner struggle to short yet revealing moments, nothing too ponderous. In other words, no protagonists navel-gazing while sitting around in their rooms, thinking about how much their life sucks. Do real-world humans—your readers—do this? Absolutely.

Especially if you're writing for middle grade and young adult audiences, your characters will whine and moan. But endless complaining isn't the best approach to conveying juicy inner struggle. Early on, let your character have a moment that encapsulates their internal tension but within the context of the opening scene. After the plot is rolling, don't stop finding opportunities to add conflict and nuance. You can even play with interiority and choices which outright contradict a reader's understanding of your protagonist. To be clear, the character's actions and reactions must be supported by specific logic that readers can follow and understand. While a protagonist won't always be rational, they must always present a *rationale*.

Sometimes, characters work to convince themselves. Other times, they're trying to convince others, including the audience. Unless protagonists intentionally "break the fourth wall" and speak directly to audiences, it's assumed they don't know they're being "watched" when they're in their own heads. Internal struggle deals a lot with appearance versus reality and whether a protagonist is especially vulnerable to "saving face" or comparing themselves to others. The prevalence of inner conflict can also depend on whether things are going well or poorly in the present action.

Showing a character's internal struggle on the page exposes readers to your protagonist's deepest self. We'll find variable self-awareness when it comes to inner conflict because characters can be more or less prepared to confront tough issues, depending on their mood, the context of the scene at hand, and where they are in their growth arcs. How a character commands their awareness of their own inner tension demonstrates their trajectory.

Opportunities to Create Inner Struggle

Many characters are designed to be smart or otherwise exceptional, which makes them interesting and engaging. Readers want a protagonist who's perceptive and capable of critical thinking. Audiences want to participate in a character's internal process, logic, and reasoning. Some genres tolerate more denial than others (like romantic denial in a romcom), but overall, if you use denial, let the character be at least somewhat aware that they're rejecting reality, then have them come around quickly. The juiciest moments of internal tension occur when a character's actions and choices conflict with their morality, value system, or true identity. Whenever we feel dissonance, especially about our inner sense of self, we will often engage in cognitive biases, magical thinking, denial, or justification to bring ourselves back into consonance. Characters do the same. Look at what many of the protagonists in the following examples do, say, and think when faced with unwelcome reality and consequences.

Unconscious Inner Struggle Text Analysis

These characters are indulging in coping mechanisms rather than confronting their true issues, wants, or needs.

The following protagonist is called out about his behavior, and his friend suggests therapy.

Example 1:

"What's going on with you?" Chaz's words hung heavy in the air. "It's obviously above my pay grade," he continued, "but I think you need help."

My throat convulsed around a response. Without looking at him, I nodded, and braced for the vertigo.

What does the character present to the world? (If you can't tell from this example, imagine what's suggested.)

_____

_____

_____

How does this clash with what's going on inside?

_____

_____

_____

Why might this split be happening?

_____

_____

_____

What does the character say or suggest they need? How might they bring themselves into consonance instead of dissonance?

_____

_____

_____

This character kisses her enemy and imagines what he might be thinking.

Example 2:

His twisted lips may be beautiful, but I can taste the venom coiled within. As our mouths meet, his is hard where it should be soft. It sets me on edge. If I didn't know any better, I'd lean in. But I do know. He's battling with himself, trying to resist the urge to give into this forbidden desire. Surely, he can't want this, or if he does, he hates himself for it.

What does the character present to the world? (If you can't tell from this example, imagine what's suggested.)

_____

_____

_____

How does this clash with what's going on inside?

_____

How does this clash with what's going on inside (cont.)?

_____

_____

Why might this split be happening?

_____

_____

What does the character say or suggest they need? How might they bring themselves into consonance instead of dissonance?

_____

_____

My Take: This one is tricky because the POV character cannot know what he's thinking. Instead, she might actually be projecting her own feelings and assigning them to her scene partner. She needs to make this kiss more "acceptable" by pretending both of them are disgusted by it, but notice that she's still choosing to proceed.

This next example comes from the writer and plagiarist we met earlier. He's loving writing now ... but something might be wrong beneath the surface.

Example 3:

I couldn't contain my happiness. The thrill of writing had finally returned. The dream I'd abandoned not a month ago now seemed tangible again. This proved it: I just needed skill and imagination and the industry would notice. That I was enough to manifest greatness.

What does the character present to the world? (If you can't tell from this example, imagine what's suggested.)

_____

_____

_____

How does this clash with what's going on inside?

_____

_____

_____

Why might this split be happening?

_____

_____

_____

What does the character say or suggest they need? How might they bring themselves into consonance instead of dissonance?

_____

_____

_____

> This low-born fantasy character is in a dangerous world and cannot display her true self because she is disguised as an heiress.

Example 4:

Though my insides are screaming, I refuse to show it. I'm someone else now, meant to embody strength and pride above all else. "I fight to win," I grit out. That's what I must say, and that's what I'll try to believe.

What does the character present to the world? (If you can't tell from this example, imagine what's suggested.)

_____

_____

_____

How does this clash with what's going on inside?

_____

_____

_____

Why might this split be happening?

_____

_____

_____

What does the character say or suggest they need? How might they bring themselves into consonance instead of dissonance?

_____

_____

_____

Conscious Inner Struggle Text Analysis

The following characters are more able to face their problems, but still struggling.

The character overleaf attempts to engage in some romantic denial but knows she's faking it. Readers might appreciate her candor.

137

Example 1:

She's not the type to casually share a train ride with a stranger, then jump to fantasizing about eating breakfast in bed together. She remains steadfast, composed—everything's fine. It's fine.

What does the character present to the world? (If you can't tell from this example, imagine what's suggested.)

_____

_____

_____

How does this clash with what's going on inside?

_____

_____

_____

Why might this split be happening?

_____

_____

_____

What does the character say or suggest they need? How might they bring themselves into consonance instead of dissonance?

_____

_____

_____

> The next character yearns to speak out about her need, but believes her partner will abandon her if she does. She diminishes herself instead.

Example 2:

My desires throttled me and I choked down what I really wanted to say. I couldn't show him the truth because he'd leave me. Enduring the pain was easy, since the alternative was actual agony.

What does the character present to the world? (If you can't tell from this example, imagine what's suggested.)

_____

_____

_____

How does this clash with what's going on inside?

_____

_____

_____

Why might this split be happening?

_____

_____

_____

What does the character say or suggest they need? How might they bring themselves into consonance instead of dissonance?

_____

What does the character say or suggest they need? How might they bring themselves into consonance instead of dissonance (cont.)?

_____

_____

> The next character develops feelings for a client, yet her workaholic tendencies get the best of her.

Example 3:

Anger and pain swirled together with the sharp sting of embarrassment. Most of all, though, was the crushing disappointment in myself for letting the mask drop with a client. Unforgivable. I vowed to never make that mistake again as I hurried to my car in full, desperate retreat.

What does the character present to the world? (If you can't tell from this example, imagine what's suggested.)

_____

_____

_____

How does this clash with what's going on inside?

_____

_____

_____

Why might this split be happening?

_____

_____

Why might this split be happening (cont.)?

_____

What does the character say or suggest they need? How might they bring themselves into consonance instead of dissonance?

_____

_____

_____

> The next character is observing two of her coworkers—Bruce and Ellen—who are having a tryst. Betty wanted Bruce for herself, yet he chose someone else. She's bitter that he seemingly has no problem cheating, yet selected a different affair partner.

Example 4:

The sight of Ellen always plunged Betty into a pit of self-doubt. She was painfully aware of her own plainness in comparison. And now, realizing that Bruce and Ellen were all wrapped up in an affair, it made her sick. Their passion was tangible, and he so very clearly belonged to her. Betty imagined Bruce eagerly leaving everything behind for his beautiful new flame. But Betty? He wouldn't even give her a second glance, let alone do the same for her.

What does the character present to the world? (If you can't tell from this example, imagine what's suggested.)

_____

_____

_____

How does this clash with what's going on inside?

_____

_____

_____

Why might this split be happening?

_____

_____

_____

What does the character say or suggest they need? How might they bring themselves into consonance instead of dissonance?

_____

_____

_____

This character manifests inner struggle in a literal way as she thinks about her new crush.

Example 5:

Her mind battled constantly, folding in on itself. Whenever they kissed, a voice inside her head would scream for her to end things immediately. Just drop out mid-kiss and run.

He's not worth it, her mind said.

But he's nice, she'd argue.

Are you sure?

Deep down, she was always dissecting her life, searching for flaws to tear into until reality became shredded by her overthinking mind.

What does the character present to the world? (If you can't tell from this example, imagine what's suggested.)

_____

_____

_____

How does this clash with what's going on inside?

_____

_____

_____

Why might this split be happening?

_____

_____

_____

What does the character say or suggest they need? How might they bring themselves into consonance instead of dissonance?

_____

_____

_____

Inner Struggle Questionnaire

01   I introduce an element of my character's inner struggle in the first chapter of my novel or memoir.

YES ☐   NO ☐

02 Does the protagonist indulge in any coping mechanisms to deal with the emotional friction of the plot?

YES ☐ NO ☐

If so, what are they?

03 Is the character acting in alignment with their values? Is their behavior consistent with the type of person they believe they are, or want to be?

YES ☐ NO ☐

How does this play out in action?

04 I know my character's general temperament and emotional baseline.

YES ☐ NO ☐

If so, describe it here:

Remember! Your character should experience variable moods, just like you do. How much bandwidth they have available to deal with tension in any moment may also fluctuate. When they have a short fuse, they're less likely to manage conflict or respond admirably. Consider, also, their general state of health. If they're sick or hindered by acute physical or mental challenges, they might not approach situations with the same mindset as usual. Don't forget that chronic issues might inform their sense of well-being, too.

05 What kind of external events or internal changes might bring your character into alignment with themselves?

Explain:

06 What might consonance feel like to them? What difference would it make in your character's life?

Explain:

Worldview

Worldview comes in many different flavors of tone and voice, and covers a wide array of ideas and beliefs. A character's expression of worldview contains a range of biases, privileges, prejudices, blind spots, sensitivities to power dynamics, perceptions of hierarchy and standing, and so much more. Worldview can also be expressed through action, dialogue, and, of course, interiority.

> **Worldview:** All protagonists have systems which govern their actions, reactions, and decisions. Worldviews encompass a character's collection of moral and personal beliefs, both important and trivial, which contribute to their personality and sense of self. These ideas can originate in any number of ways, from internal convictions to those planted by family, society, culture, and experience. Worldviews can be relatively fixed or change over time as a result of plot and character turning points

How might you convey who a character is, at their core, and what they believe? We've already considered a protagonist's backstory, sense of self, objective, motivation, need, and inner struggle, but these characterizing details don't exist in a vacuum. A worldview can certainly be influenced by one or two foundational events, but it's more likely to result from countless experiences and impressions.

Some important worldview factors:

- A character's family of origin informs their worldview (whether the protagonist hews to these ideas or rejects them is another notion);

- Friends and social circles also contribute, especially once a character begins to individuate and socialize outside of the home in adolescence;
- The larger society of the story world influences a protagonist's worldview (characters can similarly accept or reject the many explicit and implicit messages they receive on a daily basis).

Complicating matters further is the notion that worldview is a moving target, constantly changing, often subtly, but sometimes suddenly, especially following plot turning points. Worldview shifts often parallel a character's growth arc. To play with this element, you'll have to create a baseline belief system, challenge it, test it, and maybe even change it. How might worldview transform as a result? When and why could this happen? How could a value system intersect with the plot for maximum impact? Worldview is a barometer of how protagonists feel about themselves, their efforts, and their society or culture at large.

It's one thing for a writer to develop a set of worldviews for a protagonist, express them on the page, and track them over time. It's another to imagine how this element of character development affects reader engagement. When I say this, I don't mean that your reader should *agree* with your protagonist's attitudes or ways of seeing the world. In fact, compelling a reader who disagrees with your character on a fundamental level can be an exquisite writing challenge. When we create an antagonist, after all, we want audiences to relate to them, almost despite themselves.

More important than agreement is understanding, as far as the reader-character relationship is concerned. You should portray your protagonist and their static or shifting worldviews in such a way that audiences find the character and their belief systems cohesive and credible. Your goal is to help outsiders understand how a protagonist's worldview makes logical and emotional sense, whether or not they agree with the character's ideas. As with objective and motivation, a character's worldview can be productive or self-defeating, and it can either elevate them or hold them back.

I've decided to showcase some "negative" and fixed worldviews for the first round of text analysis, even though these are incredibly broad labels. Let's extrapolate what such beliefs might mean for a protagonist's identity. Then we'll look at whether a character accepts a certain worldview or rejects it. This comes into play as protagonists examine their own value systems and society's prevailing cultural wisdom. The next step is deciding whether they resonate with these established ideas. Sometimes we'll see a negative worldview which the character accepts, or a positive one they reject. There are many available permutations, and this is where you'll start to see protagonist ideas and mores in flux.

Fixed Worldview Text Analysis

Sometimes negative or fixed worldviews harm a character. Sometimes they help that protagonist get through the day.

The following character is dealing with a tough world and trying to survive. There are two worldviews here: a secondary character's is expressed; the protagonist's is implied.

Example 1:

My mom's go-to wisdom for dealing with the harsh realities of life? *Don't even think about it.* As if that's supposed to make everything better.

What is the worldview displayed here?

_____

_____

_____

How might it have arisen?

_____

How might it have arisen (cont.)?

_____

_____

How might it affect the character (good or bad)?

_____

_____

_____

| This character is grappling with growing up in end-stage capitalism. |

Example 2:

This was typical adulthood, she was gathering. You believe you'll
transform into something else, even if you don't know what, or why such
magic would look twice at you. Then reality hits, sapping your strength
until you surrender to its current and wash up on shore, where everyone
else is already in the grind, their eyes glued to screens under blinding
artificial lights, lost in the endless cycle of productivity.

What is the worldview displayed here?

_____

_____

_____

How might it have arisen?

_____

_____

_____

How might it affect the character (good or bad)?

_____

_____

_____

This character doesn't like her chances of achieving happiness, though she might also be too hard on herself.

Example 3:
I couldn't bear to look at myself, let alone accept what my life had become. Why did I dare to imagine I could have a normal life, a happy life like everyone else?

What is the worldview displayed here?

_____

_____

_____

How might it have arisen?

_____

_____

_____

How might it affect the character (good or bad)?

_____

_____

_____

This next character has kidnapped his crush's former boyfriend and locked him up. Here, he pretends to speak to his crush in **second-person direct address**, one of the less common POVs.

Example 4:

Having experienced Aaron, I have applaud you for standing him. Yeah, you might've put up with his crap, but did you ever actually lock him up and listen to his nonstop bellyaching? Trust me, I'm doing that kid a favor. He may be angry when he gets out of here, but he'll thank me eventually for turning him into a real man.

What is the worldview displayed here?

_____

_____

_____

How might it have arisen?

_____

_____

_____

How might it affect the character (good or bad)?

_____

_____

_____

Flexible Worldview Text Analysis

The following examples showcase characters who are aware of their beliefs and actively engaging with them.

This isn't necessarily a positive worldview, but it's one that might make the character's life easier. There's also an element of wish fulfillment here, as many can relate to what this protagonist expresses, even if she's joking.

Example 1:

Have no expectations. The sheer force of that idea—its stripped-down, all-encompassing freedom—was exhilarating. It was a statement you'd attribute to a self-sufficient robot, a brick wall. I longed to become just that.

What is the worldview displayed here?

_____

_____

_____

How might it have arisen?

_____

_____

_____

How might it affect the character (good or bad)?

_____

_____

How might it affect the character (cont.)?

_____

This is a sharply observed worldview statement, but it's up to you to decide whether it's a productive one. This can also be considered an **authorial aside**, since it's not necessarily in a specific character's point of view.

Example 2:

Kids see the world in a different way. Maybe it's because they're always looking up, catching us at our most unflattering angles. That's why they can be such cruel little creatures, using our weaknesses against us with lightning-fast wit. Even so, they also manage to forgive us for almost everything.

What is the worldview displayed here?

_____

_____

_____

How might it have arisen?

_____

_____

_____

How might it affect the character (good or bad)?

_____

_____

_____

Example 3:

I could easily have someone finish the job and take care of him for me, but that wouldn't be the honorable approach to settling a debt. The old ways called for a direct confrontation and a thorough airing of grievances —and if I had no traditions, I had nothing.

What is the worldview displayed here?

_____

_____

_____

How might it have arisen?

_____

_____

_____

How might it affect the character (good or bad)?

_____

_____

_____

Example 4:
Wrath ain't gonna solve nothin'. Better off lettin' it simmer and prayin' for a storm to reveal the truth.

What is the worldview displayed here?

_____

_____

_____

How might it have arisen?

_____

_____

_____

How might it affect the character (good or bad)?

_____

_____

_____

Exploring Worldview

Worldview shifts often parallel a character's growth arc. To play with this element, you'll have to create a baseline belief system, challenge it, test it, and maybe even change it by the end of your story.

Describe some aspects of your protagonist's baseline belief system:

What are some family, social, and/or other early influences which have created or contributed to this worldview?

What are some societal or cultural forces which have further shaped or contributed to the character's belief system?

What are some ways in which your character's worldview might be
challenged? Are they internal or external?

How might their worldview transform as a result? When and why could this
happen?

How might the character react to these challenges and evolutions?

Character Arc

Character growth and change are crucial for fostering reader engagement and expressing premise and theme. While the plot can entertain audiences and provide tension, conflict, and stakes, the protagonist's transformation over the course of events—relayed using action and interiority—has the power to truly reach inside the beating hearts of your readership

> **Character Arc:** A character's emotional evolution over the course of a plot. While the structure takes the protagonist through a largely external story, they are also growing (or, less commonly, regressing) in terms of identity, beliefs, values, objectives, and needs. A character arc often sees the protagonist recontextualize the past, subsume a new understanding of themselves in the present, and become more able to achieve a satisfying future.

Character growth is the figurative "journey" in the Hero's Journey and adds dimension to any literal adventure. There are some tropes and forms, like that of the anti-hero, which normalize protagonist stasis or devolution, but these exceptions are generally rare and reserved for specific categories. If you, like most writers, intend to give your protagonist a growth arc, pacing this progress is important. Ideally, you'll offer incremental benchmarks of transformation throughout. I'd strongly discourage you from writing a character who's suppressed from having any realizations until the 80% or 90% mark of the story, at which point they're struck by an epiphany. Many of the manuscripts I see in my editorial practice attempt this structure but it generally isn't satisfying. The sudden realization is also an unrealistic approach to character development. The story is the struggle. A protagonist's life won't magically become problem-free once a new understanding hits. It's naïve to believe—or to convey—that a character's existence will be smooth sailing once they have their "Eureka!" moment. Even picture book audiences are capable of understanding this nuance. Life isn't all sunshine and rainbows at the end of a story, even if the present conflict resolves relatively successfully.

The Shape of Character Arc

When it comes to character arc, writers tend to have a lot of questions. How do they convey protagonist change in a realistic and relatable way? Is the transformation too nicely wrapped up in a neat little bow at the end? Is the resolution too messy? Has the character changed too much, too little, or just enough? Is the change consistent or "out of character," and how can a writer know? Are difficult decisions made in a straightforward way or is there inner struggle? Is the growth process linear, or do characters backslide and regress before new identities, worldviews, and behaviors "stick"?

The answers to many of these questions depend on the kind of story you're writing and your characters themselves. Some genres and categories expect profound development arcs, with memoir being perhaps the most prominent, followed by literary, women's, upmarket, cozy mystery, romance, romantic comedy, and a lot of MG and YA, in no particular order.

Others are marked by flatter character arcs and less overt growth, like hardboiled mystery, thriller, suspense, horror, sci-fi, military, and action/adventure. Fantasy and speculative are broad labels, meaning you can encounter all kinds of character trajectories within these stories and their various sub-genres.

Additional Arc Pointers

- Interiority can show the walls a character has built—and the reaction when they come down.

- Wants and needs can be diametrically opposed. For example, a character needs to lose control to find themselves, yet control is what they claim to want most. Many stories are about character relationships to control, which is an inner struggle. Protagonists must either let go when grasping starts to hurt, or wrestle with building up their sense of proactive agency to gain power over their circumstances.
- The midpoint often involves a process of internal character give and take—approaching the realization, backing away, working up the courage, then meeting the situation with more resolve.
- Victories and defeats must play out on a book-length scale. Even if your character's overall trajectory is positive, it's not going to be entirely linear. Though a character is uplifted by the end, they should hit some dire emotional lows, especially during the escalating obstacles portion, and the crisis, dark night of the soul, and synthesis climax.
- An "extinction burst" refers to a behavior pattern where a maladaptive tendency flares up as a character or person realizes they can't or shouldn't continue using their current coping mechanisms. Rather than change, they up the ante on their resistance and temporarily backslide.

Single Character Arc Text Analysis

Let's check in with one example character's story-wide progression to demonstrate a growth arc in action.

This section's example character has endured a lot of negative attention because of her past, though this is only revealed later. This is her baseline when we meet her.

Example 1:

I gazed at my reflection above the dingy washbasin. There I was: Samantha, a woman who'd been scrutinized and judged her entire life. Long hair falling down my back like a waterfall. Skin as pale as a blank sheet of paper, with scars etching texture into the surface. I wanted nothing more than to escape the prying eyes and constant attention.

How is interiority used in this excerpt?

_____

_____

_____

What's it like to be this character right now?

_____

_____

_____

What kind of character growth or devolution might result from this moment?

_____

_____

_____

> She decides to pursue a new life, but incorrectly believes she'll do so by attracting a partner who is obviously wrong for her (and won't fix her anyway, because that power is within herself). This is a low point as her fantasy breaks down.

Example 2:

The man on stage was a stranger. I'd created a false reality for myself, a desperate attempt to escape my own pathetic existence. With painful clarity, I realized the futility of it all. My delusions shattered, leaving me washed up on the shores of self-hatred. The past could not be changed or erased, and I was doomed to live out my days as a solitary creature, drowning my sorrows in gin and frozen dinners. That's all I had and all I'd ever have.

How is interiority used in this excerpt?

_____

_____

_____

What's it like to be this character right now?

_____

_____

_____

What kind of character growth or devolution might result from this moment?

_____

_____

_____

The following example is rock bottom—the dark night of the soul.

Example 3:

I gulped down the gin with the determination of a sprinter, laser-focused. But no matter how much I drank, my thoughts refused to submerge again, pale in their gas-filled ugliness. Just like Mother always said, I was an embarrassment. Even my whimpers were pathetic. Why did I dare to imagine I could have a normal life, a happy life like everyone else?

How is interiority used in this excerpt?

_____

_____

How is interiority used in this excerpt (cont.)?

_____

What's it like to be this character right now?

_____

_____

_____

What kind of character growth or devolution might result from this moment?

_____

_____

_____

And this is after the synthesis climax, as she wields that power contained within herself for the first time.

Example 4:

A strange sensation washed over me. It was happiness, a feeling I had long forgotten. Just this morning, I was consumed with anger, but now I was filled with gentle sunshine. There was something stunning about the full spectrum of human emotions—their intensity, how quickly they shifted. Surprisingly, I wanted more of them. *All* of them.

How is interiority used in this excerpt?

_____

_____

_____

What's it like to be this character right now?

_____

_____

_____

What kind of character growth or devolution might result from this moment?

_____

_____

_____

Early Character Arc Text Analysis

Now let's see examples at or around various plot points to see how characters transition in their sense of self. These are early-story examples.

> This character is coming to terms with her father, who is now sick. Notice how she subsumes the flaws in their relationship as comments on herself.

Example 1:

For years, I carried the weight of my father's depression, actively making it my responsibility. But part of me still clung to the hope that I could help. The magician who could wipe away all of his pain with a wave of her hand and an easy joke.

How is interiority used in this excerpt?

_____

_____

_____

What's it like to be this character right now?

_____

_____

_____

What kind of character growth or devolution might result from this moment?

_____

_____

_____

The next character is grappling with an eating disorder early in the story.

Example 2:
She hates when people label her with cutesy adjectives. In her mind, she's nothing but a number on a scale, constantly measuring her worth against the digits on the screen. She wonders what it'd feel like to stop wanting to be less and instead to disappear altogether.

How is interiority used in this excerpt?

_____

_____

_____

What's it like to be this character right now?

_____

_____

_____

What kind of character growth or devolution might result from this moment?

_____

_____

_____

Our next character considers the duality of her public versus private persona, though she tries to explain this dissonance away by asking a philosophical question rather than truly digging deeper.

Example 3:

I was a contradiction, even to myself. In person, I presented as meek and unassuming, but online, I unleashed all my thoughts on sexism and culture without a filter. It's always awkward when someone reads my stuff, then meets me in person. I wonder who's more disappointed, them, or me. Was there even a real version of myself, or just a series of masks? Did *anyone* know who they were, though?

How is interiority used in this excerpt?

_____

_____

_____

What's it like to be this character right now?

_____

_____

_____

What kind of character growth or devolution might result from this moment?

_____

_____

_____

Midpoint(ish) Character Arc Text Analysis

And here, we see some characters at or around their pivotal midpoints.

This protagonist is reacting to a stabbing at her dorm and doesn't trust herself enough to lead, though this is expected of her.

Example 1:

I swelled with an overwhelming sense of gratitude, a desperate desire to crawl into his arms and weep. Finally, someone with training and a plan, someone who'd unravel this mess and illuminate our next steps. The relief was borderline intoxicating and I swayed where I stood.

How is interiority used in this excerpt?

_____

_____

_____

What's it like to be this character right now?

_____

_____

_____

What kind of character growth or devolution might result from this moment?

_____

_____

_____

The next character is an immigrant and feels completely lost in her new country after a setback.

Example 2:
The enormity of the world overshadowed her. In that moment, she yearned to flee back across the ocean. But she knew deep down that it wasn't just about physical distance—she carried this emptiness within her, it'd follow her wherever she went.

How is interiority used in this excerpt?

_____

_____

_____

What's it like to be this character right now?

_____

_____

_____

What kind of character growth or devolution might result from this moment?

_____

_____

What kind of character growth or devolution might result (cont.)?

_____

- -
The following character is struggling to open herself up to love.
- -

> Example 3:
>
> Love scares me. Every time I open my heart, it's only a matter of time before it's broken. Everything leads to loneliness. And I'm tired of being the one left behind, constantly picking up the pieces, trying to be whole again.

How is interiority used in this excerpt?

_____

_____

_____

What's it like to be this character right now?

_____

_____

_____

What kind of character growth or devolution might result from this moment?

_____

_____

_____

Late Character Arc Text Analysis

And here are some characters toward the end of their evolutions.

Example 1:

One day, your actions hit you like a brick to the face. You can no longer ignore the monster you've become, the lies you've told, all to keep up with everyone else. How does anyone stand who they are? How can we pretend everything's okay? As I present before my dead-eyed "team," my other self takes over, speaking on autopilot. But inside, I'm screaming, sick to see the boundaries blur between us.

How is interiority used in this excerpt?

_____

_____

_____

What's it like to be this character right now?

_____

_____

_____

What kind of character growth or devolution might result from this moment?

_____

_____

_____

When her son asks about who she is, the woman on the next page reflects on what really matters to her now that she's reaching the end of her life.

Example 2:

Had I been honest from the start, had I lived my life without restraint, he would've have truly seen *me* instead of his reliable, unremarkable mother. He loves an idealized version of me, a false one. Now I know the secret of life is to be understood.

How is interiority used in this excerpt?

_____

_____

_____

What's it like to be this character right now?

_____

_____

_____

What kind of character growth or devolution might result from this moment?

_____

_____

_____

Our last character has struggled to allow others in. This is a small moment, but it manages to deliver big stakes.

Example 3:

It doesn't matter what anyone else thinks. I can be as stupid as I want to be, I can be free. It is, actually, possible for me to enjoy myself. How had I never realized this before?

How is interiority used in this excerpt?

_____

_____

_____

What's it like to be this character right now?

_____

_____

_____

What kind of character growth or devolution might result from this moment?

_____

_____

_____

Character Arc Checklist

01	I allow my protagonist to have realizations throughout the story, not just a single epiphany at the end.	YES ☐	NO ☐
02	Is the growth process linear, or does my character backslide and regress before their new identity, worldview, and behavior "stick"?	YES ☐	NO ☐
03	My protagonist changes in a realistic and relatable way.	YES ☐	NO ☐

04   My protagonist's life doesn't magically become problem-free once a new understanding hits.   YES ☐   NO ☐

---

05   Difficult decisions involve inner struggle for my character.   YES ☐   NO ☐

---

06   The events on the story not only impact the character's moods, but their sense of worldview and identity.   YES ☐   NO ☐

---

07   The character's transformation feels earned and grounded, but also indicates a new era of their journey is about to begin.   YES ☐   NO ☐

08

My protagonist's character arc progression can best be described as:

☐ Steady forward progress

☐ Lots of ups and downs, then tragedy

☐ Lots of ups and downs, then triumph

☐ Regression or backsliding, then tragedy

☐ Regression or backsliding, then triumph

Exploring Character Arc

Your turn to apply these ideas to your character.

Describe the starting point of your protagonist's arc at the beginning:

What changes about them and their sense of identity during the escalating sequence of obstacles struggles and triumphs?

What is the big pivot in their sense of self around the midpoint, which is usually one of the most crucial times in a character's arc? (Perhaps they go from pursuing the objective to pursuing the need.)

Which parts of your character's sense of self will be tested during the crisis, which is the run-up to the bigger climax?

What must the character synthesize about themselves in the dark night of the soul and leverage to triumph during the climax (if they prevail)?

Who will the character be in the resolution and beyond?

PART THREE

SUPPORTING STORYTELLING ELEMENTS

Secondary Characters

One of the most popular questions I'm asked about non-point-of-view secondary characters is: Do I have to do the same amount of work to develop them as I do to develop my protagonist? Absolutely not. But you will want to do some thinking about their backstory, wound, objective, motivation, need, major inner struggle, worldview, and growth arc.

The next most popular question is usually: What kinds of secondary characters do I need, and how many? This, too, depends. You'll have to decide who to develop and to which degree based on your plot, genre, and target audience. Generally, humans can only sustain a handful of deep relationships at one time. You're also aiming for characters, not caricatures or stereotypes, even with your secondary cast members. If you find yourself being too broad or reductive, combine two characters, develop them more deeply, or get rid of them altogether.

All characters have the potential to get your protagonist closer to or further from their goals and needs. If a protagonist is invested in any relationship, whether positive or negative, they care. Once they're committed to something or, in this case, *someone*, everything feels elevated, each interaction seems more significant, and the outcome of scenes with that particular character matters more. Readers will start to care, too, and once a reader cares, they're hooked. Ideally, you'll design your secondary characters to lure the protagonist into backsliding, support their growth, catapult them forward, or push them backward. You should always be thinking about how a secondary character acts upon your POV character and vice versa. (Though the protagonist should also affect other cast members, this dynamic is less important unless it points back to the main character and changes their trajectory.)

Inter-character relationships offer opportunities to explore your protagonist, theme, and premise. You can also play around with your POV character's larger needs, wants, and sense of self as they perceive themselves in the context of people they know. In most cases, you'll want your secondary characters to differ from your protagonist in ways that challenge the POV, inform their sense of self or worldview, meet or subvert their needs, and otherwise create opportunities for struggle and tension. Even in a positive relationship. *Especially* in a positive relationship! Significant conflict tends to arise when characters (and humans) care about someone *more*, not less.

Theme can help dictate how these dynamics connect. For example, a protagonist who's cautious about love may be paired with a best friend who gives love freely and acts as a foil. They might also have another friend who's nursing a broken heart and providing the cautionary tale contrast. These secondary characters can change over the course of the story, but their thematically relevant and clashing individual worldviews will allow your protagonist to explore the broad idea of love with more nuance.

Character Roles

Three major roles that many secondary characters fall into are:

1. Supporters
2. Antagonists
3. Shapeshifters

Your protagonist will probably have plenty of supporters, including long-term ones like best friends or nice parents, and potential short-term ones like mentors, who come and go. Most notably, mentors and guides usually die or vanish before the climax of a more traditional Hero's Journey plot, leaving the protagonist to their own devices in a critical moment. If help is available throughout, your main character won't be or seem proactive.

The antagonist is a crucial character in many stories and deserves lavish development. Sometimes a villain will have henchmen, but they tend to be more anonymous. The exception is anyone who flips on their boss, which would be notable, and readers might want more insight into this character's background and perspective to gauge their trustworthiness. A question I hear all the time is: Does my story need an antagonist? Well, you're probably sick of hearing this non-answer but … it depends.

A thriller? Absolutely. The antagonist may even get some point-of-view chapters. A domestic thriller? Absolutely, but in this case, the antagonist is usually coming from inside the house … or at least across the street. Intergenerational literary fiction may have a more nuanced antagonist, too. It could be the family's matriarch who rules with an iron fist, but the children still love her due to a confusing blend of filial piety, cultural conditioning, and those rare golden afternoons when she seems to "snap out of it" and see beyond her disappointments, unmet needs, and impossible expectations.

Most antagonists don't think of themselves as "the bad guy." Only a disappointing and flat character gets out of bed and says, "I like power, so I'm going to do evil for the sake of evil today." This villain will be a blunt instrument, and while they might cause havoc, they won't truly play on the protagonist's or reader's psyche in any lasting or intriguing way. Most antagonists believe they're the misunderstood heroes of their own stories, at least according to their complicated worldviews, objectives, needs, or all of the above. Another question I get: What if I don't have an antagonist? All together now: It depends. But seriously, it depends on the kind of story you're writing, because not all stories have an overt villain. Tread carefully here, though. Your plot does need a reliable and escalating source of tension, conflict, and antagonism, so if you're not going to boil those down into a focal-point character, how are you going to move the narrative forward, menace your protagonist, and raise stakes?

The villain could be society itself, or a major project or undertaking. The antagonizing force could also be represented by something which exists inside the protagonist, like a dark wound or secret that's threatening to take them down from within. Long story short, you need conflict in your narrative, one way or another, but it doesn't always come from a single character (or a group of characters, led by one Big Bad).

The final broad secondary character type—shapeshifter—doesn't refer to a paranormal creature. Instead, a shape-shifting character is a combination of supporter and antagonist, someone who changes roles over the course of a story, either suddenly or along a gradual growth arc. A best friend betrays the protagonist. The antagonist saves the hero's life rather than completing the contract kill, belying their true goodness. The shapeshifter is a character whose polarity flip happens at crucial moments which coincide with plot reveals, escalations, or twists. In romance and romantic comedy, the love interest almost always plays a shapeshifter role—they start out as a wonderful supporter and potential partner, then, when vulnerable feelings threaten, they can be perceived as an antagonist. Once the lovers gain a new understanding of themselves and one another, they finally reconcile and the beloved flips into a supportive role once more.

While there are some brilliant secondary characters in shows, movies, books, and memoirs, they all have one thing in common—without the protagonist, they would be incomplete. Especially since the POV character is the lens through which audiences meet and interpret everyone else.

Rendering Secondary Characters Without Point of View Access

It's impossible to offer interiority without point-of-view access. If you can't use POV to explore someone's inner life, dialogue and action become your only available methods for conveying what a secondary character might be experiencing. There's a pretty big issue with these superficial approaches, though. All kinds of deep and unexpected stuff happens below the surface of every character, as we've learned over the last almost-200 pages. Pure showing, the domain of action and dialogue, offers readers only part of the picture. Most importantly, what's narrated, interpreted, and extrapolated about secondary characters is filtered through a protagonist's biased lens. How do writers, then, scratch at any of this complexity without interiority and point-of-view access?

- First, the secondary character can drop their mask and level with the protagonist, honestly expressing their experience. But as we've seen throughout this workbook, total authenticity and honesty prove difficult for most characters—even the self-aware ones. Also, things like worldview can shift over the course of the story, so a secondary character's earnest assessment of their feelings might be true early on but could change after a turning point.
- Second, you can have non-POV characters self-express via other means. Journals and letters are always popular as a shortcut to getting someone's "true" thoughts and feelings, but these can be manipulated. You can also have a point-of-view protagonist eavesdrop on a conversation which excludes them, though the same problem applies. The secondary character could just as easily be lying to their scene partner or omitting data, especially if they have to be careful with their information. Readers know not to take everything a non-point-of-view character—or even a POV character!—does and says at face value.
- Third, audiences can get a more nuanced—but still biased—awareness of what secondary characters are experiencing, thinking, feeling, or planning by seeing the protagonist's interpretation of these elements in interiority. As your hero goes through the story, they will be attempting to "read" other characters, just as your audience is judging and making assumptions about your protagonist. You absolutely can and should offer up your POV's interpretations and extrapolations about those around them. This information is obviously filtered through your protagonist's biases, perspectives, blind spots, and experiences. It is by no means neutral, but can be helpful in analyzing a secondary character or misleading the reader into thinking or feeling a certain way, which is common in thrillers and mysteries.

It's from this colorful web of relationships, thoughts, feelings, interpretations, reactions, expectations, and inner struggles that we create external conflict and tension between characters. If it sounds complicated, it is. Without point-of-view access, we can never truly know a non-POV character's deepest self, but rest easy, because we don't need this level of nuance. And if you find that you do want to develop a secondary character —and your story would be better and richer if readers could also intimately track their experience with interiority—consider giving them a perspective by transitioning to a multiple narrator structure.

The Mechanics of Scene

Here, I'll quickly discuss scene and dialogue, as these are a writer's available vehicles for expressing inter-character relationships. Supplement your learning with the excellent *Make a Scene* by Jordan Rosenfeld and *Dialogue* by Robert McKee.

Scene is your opportunity to show off what your secondary characters want and why. It's also a great chance to stymie your protagonist, throw obstacles in their way, and make them dig deep to attempt various actions and strategies. Protagonists should have an objective, motivation, and expectation at the beginning of every scene. Then they'll play actions to (ideally) achieve the goal, and react in the moment as the objective is frustrated, obstacles arise, or secondary characters introduce conflict and and tension. External struggle can also come from the story world and apply pressure to the proceedings. Interiority is very useful for rendering character reactions as protagonists seek to understand what their scene partner is doing, think about what lies beneath their façade, and otherwise gear up for their next gambit or decision. New information is interpreted, meaning is extrapolated and maybe even subsumed, and the scene puts your protagonist's sense of self into action. The POV character can be honest with others, or they can intentionally mislead, pretend, or play on their scene partner's perceived vulnerabilities and misbeliefs. What's said and done in scene shouldn't be purely literal. Consider how you might introduce subtext and nuance to everyone's behavior.

After a scene is over, the protagonist can unpack what happened, choose a different plan of attack (literal or figurative) going forward, and decide what this means for their objective or need. A polarity shift is also welcome as the POV character goes from excitement to defeat, or vice versa. This pattern reinforces the story's cause-and-effect logic, as one scene leads to another, taking previous events into consideration, and so on, and so forth.

Secondary Character Text Analysis

Let's see some protagonist interpretation of non-POV characters in action.

> A hilarious characterization seen by a protagonist.

Example 1:

Their mother had no instinct for cooking. She inched into the kitchen like a bomb defuser. Her attempts at pasta were always by the box, but somehow still ended up either too mushy or burnt to a crisp. Casseroles were a disaster. But Southern society's pressure was unrelenting, and she persisted in her culinary failures every time a glossy magazine came out with a new slate of recipes.

What does this interiority seem to say about the secondary character?

_____

_____

_____

What's the protagonist's take on them?

_____

_____

_____

What kind of conflict or camaraderie is inherent in this relationship?

_____

_____

_____

Example 2:
This love was foreign to me, unnatural. I showed my mother affection out of dread, like a faithful follower groveling to avoid getting thunderstruck. But as [my new girlfriend] professed her love, I couldn't help believing her. It was a new kind of devotion, one not rooted in fear.

What does this interiority seem to say about the secondary character?

_____

_____

_____

What's the protagonist's take on them?

_____

_____

_____

What kind of conflict or camaraderie is inherent in this relationship?

_____

_____

_____

Example 3:

I mull over the situation. Dad's "peace at any price" act is falling apart, not that he'd admit it. Part of me wants to experience what it's like to stop pretending. But I don't trust him as an ally yet—he always runs back to Mom.

What does this interiority seem to say about the secondary character?

_____

_____

_____

What's the protagonist's take on them?

_____

_____

_____

What kind of conflict or camaraderie is inherent in this relationship?

_____

_____

A classic fantasy antagonist portrait, as seen by the protagonist.

Example 4:

Once again, I'm stuck sitting next to Aurora. The glint of silverware on the table makes me anxious—in Aurora's hands, the knives are nothing but instruments of torture. Every time she picks up the serrated edge, my muscles tighten, anticipating the sting. Aurora catches my eye and smiles. It's like she knows the exact effect she has on me, and enjoys every moment.

What does this interiority seem to say about the secondary character?

_____

_____

_____

What's the protagonist's take on them?

_____

_____

_____

What kind of conflict or camaraderie is inherent in this relationship?

_____

_____

_____

Character Relationship Text Analysis

These samples show some protagonist interpretations of their relationships.

Another fraught mother/daughter bond with a surprising conclusion from the protagonist. Unfortunately, she turns her back on the solution she's reached.

Example 1:

I used to sit there while she slept, hands tucked under the pillow, looking so much like a child afraid of the dark. In those moments, I couldn't blame her for anything—it wasn't her fault she'd never learned to love in the first place. *I'll be a better daughter, show her kindness, break the chain.* But it was easier said than done, especially when she was awake.

What does this interiority seem to say about the relationship?

_____

_____

_____

What's the protagonist's take on them?

_____

_____

_____

What kind of conflict or camaraderie is inherent in this relationship?

_____

_____

_____

> A potential new friendship hits the rocks because of the POV character's perception of the other woman, who happens to be a therapist in training, and her intentions.

Example 2:

The realization cut through me like a searing backhand. She claimed that helping other women was her life's calling. But in this moment, it became painfully clear. She didn't want to be my friend; she wanted to practice on me because I was such a lost cause.

What does this interiority seem to say about the relationship?

_____

_____

What does this interiority seem to say about the relationship (cont.)?

_____

_____

What's the protagonist's take on them?

_____

_____

_____

What kind of conflict or camaraderie is inherent in this relationship?

_____

_____

_____

Love relationships are a category in and of themselves because they have the power to truly activate and heal a protagonist (or plunge them into the depths of despair). This example expresses the highest potential of love.

Example 3:

He forgot how to cry after his brother died. Instead, he'd bottled up his emotions, fearing they would only bring him down if he unleashed them. Vulnerability was a taint he couldn't afford. But now he longed to release these pent-up burdens and start anew. All he could do was hope she would embrace him—baggage, and all.

What does this interiority seem to say about the relationship?

_____

_____

_____

What's the protagonist's take on them?

_____

_____

_____

What kind of conflict or camaraderie is inherent in this relationship?

_____

_____

> And here, a spouse rages when his wife runs off, leaving him to pick up the
> pieces of a family rupture.

Example 4:

His fury is a monstrous force, tearing through him like a beast unleashed.
He wants to scream at his wife, wherever she may be. To demand
answers. To remind her that she's not the victim here. That now she's
something closer to the perpetrator. He thrums with the urge to grab the
sturdy chair beneath him and fling it against the wall, picturing the
satisfying crash as it splinters. *Where are you? Answer me!*

What does this interiority seem to say about the relationship?

_____

_____

What's the protagonist's take on them?

_____

_____

What's the protagonist's take on them (cont.)?

_____

What kind of conflict or camaraderie is inherent in this relationship?

_____

_____

_____

Build Your Cast

Now it's your turn to identify some juicy secondary characters.

CHARACTER #1 NAME: _____

Some characterizing details about them:

Which category does this character fall into?

☐ Supporter (positive relationship)

☐ Antagonist (negative relationship)

☐ Shapeshifter (relationship evolves throughout the story)

How does this secondary character affect the protagonist?

CHARACTER #2 NAME: _____

Some characterizing details about them:

Which category does this character fall into?

☐ Supporter (positive relationship)

☐ Antagonist (negative relationship)

☐ Shapeshifter (relationship evolves throughout the story)

How does this secondary character affect the protagonist?

CHARACTER #3 NAME: _____

Some characterizing details about them:

Which category does this character fall into?

☐ Supporter (positive relationship)

☐ Antagonist (negative relationship)

☐ Shapeshifter (relationship evolves throughout the story)

How does this secondary character affect the protagonist?

CHARACTER #4 NAME: _____

Some characterizing details about them:

Which category does this character fall into?

☐ Supporter (positive relationship)

☐ Antagonist (negative relationship)

☐ Shapeshifter (relationship evolves throughout the story)

How does this secondary character affect the protagonist?

Who affects the protagonist the most and why?

Information Reveals

As protagonists begin to interface with your intended structure, they learn information, react to events, make decisions, and otherwise move through the larger story. How you deploy data affects plot, character, relationships, and how protagonists advance their objectives, needs, and arcs. If you think about it, all stories are crafted from a sequence of reveals. How you parcel out information depends on the kind of book you're writing. Does your intended project benefit from a slow build to a climactic twist? There are upsides and downsides to this approach.

If readers are offered too few details to make them engaged throughout the plot, they might not stick around until the very end. Intrigue doesn't develop from the total absence of information, after all. It's created by withholding crucial details. Mysteries and thrillers often present an abundance of clues and red herrings, but it's not until a single new angle or data point is introduced late in the story that everything snaps into place or rearranges into a surprising configuration.

Your decision to present audiences and characters with information throughout your story can be a powerful way to manipulate reader experience, which should be one of your primary goals. As you write, you'll need to come up with data points and escalating revelations because your character requires inputs to react to, interpret, and consider as they make decisions. A word of caution here about body language. Some writers really try to put a lot of information into a glance or tilt of the head. The protagonist then interprets this through interiority and arrives at an oddly specific (and, usually, correct) conclusion. That's asking a lot of a gesture or tone of voice. It's also disengaging to readers, similar to a character deciding something out of the blue or simply knowing the solution to a problem. Let audiences into a protagonist's critical thinking process instead of keeping them at arm's length. Our examples in this chapter focus on characters getting and reacting to information.

Information Reveals Text Analysis

Let's see how protagonists interface with data.

Here's a character "simply knowing" that danger has found her. I don't love this approach, but the below is an effective example.

> ### Example 1:
>
> A sense of familiarity and primal fear rises within her. Like a moth licked by its first-ever flame, she instinctively knows to flee. It's as if her bones sense the enemy before her mind can fully comprehend it.

How is interiority used in this excerpt?

_____

_____

_____

What might the significance of this information be?

_____

_____

_____

How might this moment affect or change things for the character?

_____

How might this moment affect or change things for the character (cont.)?

_____

_____

This description contains foreshadowing, as this character does, eventually, drown. It's also an interesting characterizing detail before readers know the outcome.

Example 2:

She'd always been at odds with the pool. While everyone else relaxed around one, it set her teeth on edge. Every night, she forced herself to swim, determined to conquer the crippling fear that she'd one day drown.

How is interiority used in this excerpt?

_____

_____

_____

What might the significance of this information be?

_____

_____

_____

How might this moment affect or change things for the character?

_____

_____

_____

The following two examples come from a multi-POV thriller story where we see two married characters interpreting each other. The wife is having an affair, and soon, we see her husband's perspective on the same scene. (As you read these, consider whether you think Bruce, the affair partner, is guilty of the murder in question. These examples attempt to steer the reader's impression, too.)

Example 3: Ellen

Her husband's gaze burns into her, a glint of malice in his eyes. Panic sets in as she wonders if he knows about her and Bruce. How did he figure it out? Is he enjoying this turn of events? Has he been following the news? She can sense his anger simmering just beneath the surface.

Example 4: Chuck

His gaze shifts to his wife, who looks tense as she stares at the flickering television screen. Ellen must be devastated to know she stooped to blowing up their marriage over a child murderer. To realize you've been in love with a monster. Well, she deserves every ounce of pain she feels.

How is interiority used in Ellen's excerpt?

_____

_____

_____

How is interiority used in Chuck's excerpt?

_____

_____

_____

What might the significance of this information be for Ellen?

_____

_____

_____

What might the significance of this information be for Chuck?

_____

_____

_____

How might this moment affect or change things for Ellen?

_____

_____

_____

How might this moment affect or change things for Chuck?

_____

_____

_____

Information Reveals Checklist

01   I reveal plot- and character-relevant
      information to characters and readers   YES   NO
      at regular intervals. (No passive   ☐   ☐
      protagonists here!)

02   If I'm working in a genre that hinges on shocking twists (like mystery/thriller), I've tried to present 80% of the information and withold the most incendiary 20%.   YES ☐   NO ☐

03   Unless I'm writing high-octane thriller or a climactic sequence, I don't end every chapter on a cliffhanger (readers grow numb to this after a while).   YES ☐   NO ☐

04   My protagonist does not make decisions with no information ("just knowing"). I use interiority to track their impressions, thought processes, and conclusions instead.   YES ☐   NO ☐

05   I use foreshadowing whenever possible to plant seeds for future events, but try to do this subtly.   YES ☐   NO ☐

06   My character reactions and interpretations/extrapolations of information are seen through the POV's unique perspective and lens.   YES ☐   NO ☐

07   I consider how information leads and potentially misleads the reader.   YES ☐   NO ☐

Reactions and Decisions

You now have an entire arsenal at your disposal for creating meaning with interiority. How your protagonist interfaces with your plot will, in turn, help readers make meaning from your story. The importance of character reactions cannot be overstated. Whether the input is big or small, you can generate energy around any stimulus. First, you must decide what matters. Then let characters clock it, too. Finally, you can use interiority to show when and how your protagonist reacts to action and information. This is key to enhancing the protagonist-story connection.

A character's reaction to events is the foundation for developing stakes and tension while also juicing as much conflict and emotion as possible from the plot. Nuanced reactions at important moments make the story resonate at a higher frequency and help readers track the cause-and-effect logic of any identity evolution your protagonist might experience. When you put a POV protagonist into action, your job is to show them reflecting on their scene partners, interpreting situations, making assumptions, and extracting meaning from events. This is interiority in a nutshell. Protagonists can then use their insights—whether correct or not—to make progress in the plot and within relationships. Reactions should happen in every scene, but sometimes you'll want to dig deeply into especially consequential ones—which I call turning points.

> **Turning Point:** The ultimate intersections of character, arc, plot, and relationship. ... (*cont.*)

Turning Point (cont.): Turning points include the major tentpole moments, but can also refer to scenes where characters address wounds, shift worldviews, abandon superficial objectives, change relationship dynamics, or experience revelations. Compelling turning points can also trigger subsumation and growth. A protagonist's interiority—thoughts, feelings, reactions, expectations, and inner struggles—at important junctures can absolutely make these moments land on both characters and readers with maximum emotional impact.

Your goal is to craft a story that maintains momentum throughout by making and manipulating meaning. When readers see protagonists faced with obstacles and reacting according to where they are in their growth arcs, audiences become and stay invested.

The Interiority of Character Reactions

Our goal, as writers, is to make readers care, create meaning, and connect character, plot, and theme. Once we're comfortable in your understanding of what interiority is and how it's used to convey character experience, we can examine some instances of big decisions and how those showcase a story's stakes. Once a character makes a choice in the plot or about their sense of self, there may not be an opportunity to reverse it. New decisions and options flow from the previous turning point. What's decided might be celebrated or regretted in hindsight, but it has become woven into the story, either way. This is especially true of turning points and one-way doors, like the inciting incident, after which there's truly no going back to the character's previous life or frame of mind. Storytelling means you're always applying conflict and tension to your protagonist, and this might push them to jettison their misbeliefs, temporarily doubt themselves, redouble their efforts, or all of the above. Decisions are powerful benchmarks in any novel or memoir. The last thing you want to do is craft an entirely linear plot with no opportunities for your character to make mistakes, reckon with their actions, and choose the wrong option. Characters (and humans) often vacillate, especially when faced with serious choices or major potential consequences. They weigh various outcomes and sometimes even experience instant regret or the urge to flee, whether or not they act on it. As we know, it's common for characters to revisit memories and imagine how things might've turned out differently. This isn't a sign of weakness, either. In fact, it's a very relatable trait—a mark of self-awareness and humanity. Just don't do it constantly, and let the most important decisions "stick," so you can avoid outright flip-flopping.

> **Flip-Flopping:** The undesirable tendency for characters to go back and forth to opposing extremes rather than committing to any one decision. An example would be a protagonist in an enemies-to-lovers romance claiming to hate their crush, then love them, then hate them again without turning point moments in between (which help readers track the character's wildly shifting feelings). Every change of heart should be motivated by the plot and contextualized with interiority to express the logic of the protagonist's new position.

There's Always a Choice

First, you should engineer difficult choices into your story. If a decision is simple, there's no emotion or sacrifice involved. The character's next move is predictable and nobody cares. Protagonists show who they are in part with the choices they make. Put characters to the test and don't let them get away too easily, especially when they're at important turning points or plot tentpoles.

Second, you want the character to make intentional decisions rather than acting without thinking. Sure, they might have moments of impulsivity, but at crucial junctures—buying into a conflict with the antagonist, declaring feelings to their crush—don't have them simply blurt things automatically. Make them consider the pros and cons, or imagine the potential ramifications, then choose to do the hard thing. Blurting is storytelling cowardice. It absolves a character of accountability. It's also important to avoid what is sometimes called "jumping conflict," or a skip between logical steps. Use interiority to ground readers in why a character makes a specific choice or reacts a certain way. Excluding the audience and simply jumping to a decision or action can feel alienating or, worse, like a plot hole or "out of character" moment. Remember—protagonists may not always be rational, but they'll each have their own *rationale*.

Finally, there's always a choice. I cannot tell you how often I pick up a manuscript (and sometimes even a published book) and read some variation of, "He had no choice." This is false. **There is always a choice**. The character might not like the menu of available options, but there is always something they can do, as long as they are still alive, to try and tilt the odds in their favor or escape a situation.

Character Reaction Text Analysis

Now we'll see these ideas in action.

> Here, a character sees her ex-boyfriend and best friend kissing, but seems more upset that it's happening at work (which shows her priorities).

Example 1:

It was like watching a train wreck in slow motion, only this time it involved my ex and so-called best friend sucking face. Worse, they had the gall to do it on the job. I couldn't rip my eyes away, couldn't figure out how to stop this from happening. Was this some cruel prank? Nope, they obviously weren't thinking. Not about me, anyway.

How is interiority used in this excerpt?

_____

_____

_____

What might the significance of this moment be?

_____

_____

Based on this reaction, how might the character now be affected?

_____

_____

This character is forced to pretend she's a member of the court in a fantasy world. The prince has done her a favor and rescued her from the draft but this doesn't make her new existence any easier. Here, she's officially presented to the prince and they both have to play their public roles.

Example 2:

The servants part like a faceless sea, allowing me to stumble to the back of the receiving line. He was the one who offered me this position, who rescued me from certain death. But he is not just anyone. He is royalty. Crown royalty. The very figurehead everyone here worships, and everyone back home despises.

How is interiority used in this excerpt?

_____

_____

What might the significance of this moment be?

_____

What might the significance of this moment be (cont.)?

_____

_____

Based on this reaction, how might the character now be affected?

_____

_____

_____

Character Decision Text Analysis

> The following comes from a second-chance romance story, where a woman must decide whether to reunite with her ex-husband after a nasty divorce.

Example 1:

Can I bear the agony of giving in just once, knowing I'll always crave him? My body aches for the pleasure I know we're capable of. I wounded him, but he can wound me back with just one touch. He can destroy me. I'd welcome it. Perhaps if we'd talked back then, things would be different now. But it's too late for regret. As it turns out, I'm willing to ruin myself completely for one more night together.

How is interiority used in this excerpt?

_____

_____

_____

What might the significance of this moment be?

_____

_____

_____

Based on this decision, how might the character now be affected?

_____

_____

_____

This character agrees to be deported rather than fighting the process.
There's dialogue here, yes, but note the interiority.

Example 2:

His voice trembled as he spoke. "Fine, I'll leave. No contest." The last shred of his pride slipped away like a torn wrapper, leaving him exposed.
The lawyer's expression shifted from apathy to surprise. "Really?" She hastily got up from her desk, relieved at the lighter caseload. She could simply check off a box, indicating her client would be willingly deported.
The word echoed mercilessly, making him feel like an object. Something to be discarded.

How is interiority used in this excerpt?

_____

_____

_____

What might the significance of this moment be?

_____

What might the significance of this moment be (cont.)?

_____

_____

Based on this decision, how might the character now be affected?

_____

_____

_____

This is from a thriller. A father was the last person to see his missing daughter. Here's the moment he chooses to lie to police during an interrogation, which will damn him.

Example 3:

He's painfully aware that she was home earlier, letting herself in with the spare key. He saw her, hit her. Disgust churns within him, but he can't let it show. He steels himself, then suggests, "Maybe she took a walk. Got lost."

How is interiority used in this excerpt?

_____

_____

_____

What might the significance of this moment be?

_____

_____

_____

Based on this decision, how might the character now be affected?

_____

_____

_____

In a historical wartime story, the following character has decided to kill an enemy soldier who the command has placed in her home. Here's how she prepares to take an action which might get her executed.

Example 4:

Regret echoed in her mind as she slipped the sedative into her daughter's drink. Bringing Stella was impossible, so was leaving her alone. Nothing but bad options these days. As she waited for the drug to take effect, she paced restlessly, every sound amplified in the stillness of the old house. Finally, as evening fell, she donned her husband's old overalls and went out to the garden where she'd told the captain to meet her.

How is interiority used in this excerpt?

_____

_____

_____

What might the significance of this moment be?

_____

_____

_____

Based on this decision, how might the character now be affected?

_____

Based on this decision, how might the character now be affected (cont.)?

_____

_____

Reactions and Decisions Checklist

01	Throughout my story, there are opportunities for the protagonist to react to events.	YES ☐	NO ☐
02	Reactions are used to steer the plot and suggest character change.	YES ☐	NO ☐
03	I've engineered difficult choices for my protagonist whenever possible.	YES ☐	NO ☐
04	My character makes intentional decisions, instead of acting on impulse.	YES ☐	NO ☐
05	My character decisions do not skip between logical steps. I use interiority to portray the reasoning behind them.	YES ☐	NO ☐
06	There is no instance of "He/She/They had no choice."	YES ☐	NO ☐
07	My protagonist makes difficult choices that go against their worldview.	YES ☐	NO ☐

If so, what are they?

_____

Leveraging Stakes

Once we unlock the power of reactions and decisions, it's all about the stakes, baby. The bloodier the better. Actually, that's not true at all, as we'll see in some excerpts that manage to load small moments with major perceived significance.

> **Stakes:** Why a development, reaction, decision, action, or idea matters. Stakes make meaning. Why is this story element important to the protagonist? How might it change their internal or external trajectory? Did they get what they wanted? And? So? Did they fail? And? So? Routinely ask these questions as you use interiority to show how characters interpret, extrapolate, and even subsume your plot's events and define their impact. This is how readers understand the ramifications of various experiences on your character's sense of self, which is where you can explore the most profound stakes of all.

Stakes enhance moments of plot and character intersection. They emerge as a result of need and want, can be positive or negative (more on that in a moment), lead to or result from decisions, anchor a moment or reaction, eliminate or create options for the future, and are often held together with cause-and-effect logic and interiority.

My favorite questions of "And? So?" are useful for teasing out stakes. They can help you imagine what the best-case and worst-case scenarios are for any plot or character development. Turning points offer major opportunities to combine growth arc, plot, and character relationships. These events are only impactful if you define their stakes and have protagonists use interiority to anticipate them before, react to them during, interpret them after, or all of the above.

Writers often take it too easy on their characters. This section reminds you to make tension ever-present by using interiority as your secret weapon. Information reveals, reactions, decisions, and stakes can also rescue your muddy middle. The writer's job in this long stretch of manuscript is to use protagonist growth, plot action, and relationship development to pick up the slack. There are many opportunities for a book to droop and interiority must be threaded through every event to make sure readers stay engaged. Focusing on stakes in key narrative moments can keep readers turning pages. Don't just think about the scene you want to write, consider when and where it can create maximum impact in your structure. Of course, you can also tease out the stakes of small moments, as you'll see in some of the following examples.

Small Stakes Text Analysis

Let's see the power of interiority to enhance stakes, even when the external stimuli doesn't seem too consequential.

> A rule-following woman disengages from a social interaction. She has never allowed herself to act this way before.

Example 1:

The drone of smalltalk fades into the background. And in that moment, she makes a decision. That woman is of no concern to her. She'll simply ... walk away. And she does, feeling freedom wash over her. Just like that.

How is interiority used in this excerpt?

How is interiority used in this excerpt (cont.)?

_____

_____

Why does this moment matter (internally)?

_____

_____

_____

How might the character be affected going forward?

_____

_____

_____

The following character has taken a big gamble by stealing his dead friend's manuscript. There's very little plot in this moment, but the stakes manage to feel larger than life.

Example 2:

Giving up writing would be the death of me. My fingers would forever ache to feel the smooth spines of books in a store, and my mind would torture itself, imagining the work each title took behind the scenes. And every time someone landed a book deal or some fresh-faced prodigy got to live out my dream, I'd hate myself even more.

How is interiority used in this excerpt?

_____

_____

How is interiority used in this excerpt (cont.)?

_____

Why does this moment matter (internally)?

_____

_____

_____

How might the character be affected going forward?

_____

_____

_____

Speculative Stakes Text Analysis

Fantasy and adventure stories involve a lot of potential danger, external conflict, and big emotional ramifications.

The following character is fighting for his town against a monster. This is also a good example of how to portray the feeling of having magic (we'll talk more about world-building in a little bit). We also slip into the antagonist's perspective to contextualize its reaction.

Example 1:

This is our town. Not yours. I unleash my full power, feeling the beast writhe and shudder beneath my heel, spewing iridescent streams across the city. It recoils—nobody's been brave enough to cause it pain in centuries. It retaliates with lightning speed, catching me off guard. From a hidden realm, a tentacle the size of a skyscraper crashes into the harbor.

How is interiority used in this excerpt?

_____

_____

_____

Why does this moment matter (internally)?

_____

_____

_____

How might the character be affected going forward?

_____

_____

_____

Up next, a character spots an undead being. Notice the suspenseful pacing.

Example 2:

She drew closer to him, all of her senses heightened, searching. Slowly, she stopped and listened. There was nothing within him, no signs of life pulsing through his veins, no familiar bodily rhythms beneath his skin. Even his breaths felt hollow and mechanical, like each one was a conscious choice. It was as if a perfect replica had been molded from clay, but without the final, vital spark of life. He looked the part, yet was disturbingly incomplete.

How is interiority used in this excerpt?

_____

How is interiority used in this excerpt (cont.)?

_____

_____

Why does this moment matter (internally)?

_____

_____

_____

How might the character be affected going forward?

_____

_____

_____

High Stakes Text Analysis

Let's see how interiority is used to underscore dangerous events, including death itself (but in an unexpected way).

This is the moment a character realizes her mother is finally dead of a cancer that'd threatened for a long time. Notice how the typical clichés of hair-rending and wailing are missing. The stakes are high, but the character's reaction helps keep the moment grounded instead of veering into melodrama.

Example 1:

Mom wasn't sleeping. Her face was strangely smooth. It was unlike Mom to be this calm. I resisted the urge to slap her awake for leaving me here.

How is interiority used in this excerpt?

_____

_____

_____

Why does this moment matter (internally)?

_____

_____

_____

How might the character be affected going forward?

_____

_____

_____

This character is in the grips of an eating disorder. Here, she gives into a binge and the interiority really makes the danger hit home.

Example 2:

As she chewed and swallowed, a strange numbness overtook her. She could almost disconnect from her body. The sugary sweetness on her tongue and the smooth glide down her throat kept her anchored to reality, but just barely. *What am I doing? What am I doing? What am I doing?* She gasped for air yet kept eating.

How is interiority used in this excerpt?

_____

_____

How is interiority used in this excerpt (cont.)?

_____

Why does this moment matter (internally)?

_____

_____

_____

How might the character be affected going forward?

_____

_____

_____

Stakes Checklist

		YES	NO
01	I've completed the "And? So?" exercise to establish any missing stakes.	☐	☐
02	Stakes exist in my story on both a grand, story-wide scale and a smaller, day-to-day scale.	☐	☐
03	I'm able to point to stakes in every chapter and scene.	☐	☐
04	As I'm writing and revising, I'm asking myself: Why does **this** matter?	☐	☐
05	I create stakes by going back to a character's sense of objective and—especially—need.	☐	☐
06	If I don't find stakes, I cut or revise the scene in question.	☐	☐

Story World

Many fantasy, speculative, sci-fi, and historical novels must do more telling, especially early on, simply because the writer needs to flesh out a time period, location, and set of magical or scientific rules (if applicable). But make no mistake: A contemporary realistic book set in the current time and a recognizable place needs world-building, too. A rural setting differs from an urban one, and nepo babies can have very different perspectives on the same piece of property compared to the landscaper's kids who live in the carriage house.

Interiority is very useful in establishing this kind of context, defining the rules of the world, and, best of all, helping characters reflect on how their environments affect and inform their sense of self. You don't have to be hindered by "write what you know" when it comes to world-building. Yes, your experiences and culture obviously inform your writing on a general level. But you can expand beyond your setting horizons, especially if you're writing a speculative story, by leveraging research and imagination.

Historical is a major genre which requires intense world-building. Sometimes your narrative will stick closely to what you're able to learn from first-person accounts. Other times, a premise will take some liberties by imagining what a well-known historical person's life might have been like behind closed doors, or use a speculative or revisionist approach, as Colson Whitehead does in *The Underground Railroad.* Intention is important here. Why are you tweaking history? Whose story are you telling? What is your objective in telling this story in this way? Is it to shine a light on an undiscovered or unexamined historical figure or time period? Is it to find an imaginative way to dramatize a social movement or the ramifications of a prevailing narrative?

Shifting over to fantasy and science fiction, imagine how your world-building affects your protagonist. Not all speculative stories feature characters with special abilities—or who can interface with powerful creatures or technology—but many do. These powers can be granted, earned, wielded with a spell or object, or innate, and it's especially interesting to meet a protagonist when their own magic awakens (or doesn't), or a character who represents an exception to an established rule.

While fantasy and science fiction stories have alternative universal laws and magic guidelines, our realistic world has cultures and family systems, and these still need definition. Early in a story, the familial worldview is often the accepted status quo, and nobody is actively rebelling against or trying to change it. This means there's room for a personal growth arc which sees the protagonist separate from their family of origin. Later, the character is subject to the forces which shape their worldview, as we saw—social relationships, the culture at large, and the setting, too. Every story world is distinct. For our purposes, I've divided our examples into those with a more realistic setting and those which showcase speculative and historical world-building.

Realistic World-Building Text Analysis

The character below is talking about her sister, who has left home and lost touch with the volatile family system.

Example 1:

But Cookie was never trained to predict the storms Mom generates. Since she moved out, I've shielded her from the full force of my mother's wrath, making excuses for why she can't attend family gatherings and distracting Cookie when Mom is in one of her moods. It's my own doing, really, that she remains oblivious to what looms over us all.

How is interiority used in this excerpt?

_____

_____

_____

What do you glean about the story world?

_____

_____

_____

How does this reflect on the character as well?

_____

_____

_____

The setting and world can also mirror the character's emotional state, which happens in the following example.

Example 2:

But I know that if I plead with him, poisoning the air inside the car, he'll veer off course, driving for hours into the depths of the brackish lowlands, farther away from civilization. The wind pummels the windows, the tires kick up gravel, stirring up a frenzy of dust and debris. We hold each other, pretending there's nothing in the rearview mirror.

How is interiority used in this excerpt?

_____

_____

221

How is interiority used in this excerpt (cont.)?

_____

What do you glean about the story world?

_____

_____

_____

How does this reflect on the character as well?

_____

_____

_____

> The final character in this realistic selection has immigrated to America and perceives her new world according to smell.

Example 3:

The scent of history lingered in Pittsburgh, a musty reminder of the past. Mystic reeked of neglect, while Richmond boasted a briny aroma, and Queens emitted the stench of sun-warmed garbage. But Trenton? There was nothing to smell here, just clean, fresh air. She relished breathing here and feeling at ease.

How is interiority used in this excerpt?

_____

_____

_____

What do you glean about the story world?

_____

_____

_____

How does this reflect on the character as well?

_____

_____

_____

Speculative World-building Text Analysis

The next character must pretend she's an heiress but doesn't trust that the courtiers will accept her. She sees danger everywhere.

Example 1:

The maids yank and twist, molding me to fit a stranger's dress. It's a grim makeover for my impending death. I'm no princess, and my people never marry up. The crown will never touch my head. Mark my words, they have other plans for me, perhaps an "accident," or "spoiled" food. Deceit has lifted me to these heights, but it will dash me back down to earth, too.

How is interiority used in this excerpt?

_____

_____

_____

What do you glean about the story world?

_____

What do you glean about the story world (cont.)?

_____

_____

How does this reflect on the character as well?

_____

_____

_____

> The next character lives in a fantasy world of mob-like ruling families. He's
> the new leader of one but struggles with the expectations of the role. He
> imagines getting rid of the previous leader—his grandfather—and, by
> extension, his old ideas. (Backstory: The protagonist's wife has just left him,
> and Grandfather is displeased that he hasn't lashed out at her lover.)

Example 2:

The abhorrent thought of pushing his grandfather out of the window flitted
through his mind. Was that what the old man craved? Arrogant, ruthless
violence? Would doing so make him more of a man? He grimaced,
knowing he could have challenged her lover to a brutal fight, hastened his
death, the way any honorable leader would. But it'd have been senseless. A
hollow victory. He couldn't force her to stay if she was already set on
leaving, and all he'd achieve was her hatred. If you truly loved someone,
shouldn't their happiness matter above all else, even your pride?

How is interiority used in this excerpt?

_____

_____

_____

What do you glean about the story world?

_____

_____

_____

How does this reflect on the character as well?

_____

_____

_____

Historical World-building Text Analysis

This colonial-era character is reacting to the untouched beauty of her surroundings and worrying whether the woods will retain their essence once civilization descends.

Example 1:

She gazed upon the endless expanse of trees, where birds flitted from branch to branch and sunlight filtered through the foliage. But instead of feeling joy, she couldn't help a twinge of sadness, knowing her people would rather see this paradise as something to be colonized, the streets filled with clanging metal and smoke, darkening the horizon.

How is interiority used in this excerpt?

_____

_____

_____

What do you glean about the story world?

_____

_____

_____

How does this reflect on the character as well?

_____

_____

_____

This is a modern character, so I'm cheating a bit by selecting this example, but he's imagining what the prairie used to be like. Plus, it pairs very nicely with the previous example. History can be established in contrast to the present, informing both time periods.

Example 2:

He strains to conjure up the image of America's prairie before it was ravaged by the farms. He yearns for waves of tall grass, towering over him and licking in the summer breeze, an endless view in every direction. And now, all of it lies destroyed. As he gazes out at what was once the Bluestem Pasture, he wonders if jaded travelers call this place a "flyover" because they don't care to face what they'd done.

How is interiority used in this excerpt?

_____

_____

_____

What do you glean about the story world?

_____

_____

_____

How does this reflect on the character as well?

_____

_____

_____

World-building Checklist

| 01 | The world has a specific setting, which informs both story and character. | YES ☐ | NO ☐ |

| 02 | I've used descriptions to evoke emotions and provide information. | YES ☐ | NO ☐ |

| 03 | There's a pervasive sense of the culture, social values, and overall atmosphere. | YES ☐ | NO ☐ |

| 04 | The world elements have an impact on the protagonist and vice versa. | YES ☐ | NO ☐ |

| 05 | The set-up of the world intentionally introduces a sense of conflict and stakes for the protagonist, secondary characters, and antagonist(s)—this is not a conflict-free place to be. | YES ☐ | NO ☐ |

06 The logic of the speculative or historical world (if applicable) is clear —there are rules, they make sense, and their boundaries and parameters shape the plot and directly affect the characters, especially the POV.

YES ☐   NO ☐

07 The world-building involves elements of power dynamics and hierarchies, placing the character either inside or outside of the prevailing structure.

YES ☐   NO ☐

Take a moment to define any important world-building elements that you want to keep in mind, such as technology (or lack thereof); magic and other powers/abilities (if applicable); social structure; religion, faith, and myth; the history of the world in question; how society has evolved to where it is now and the world's sense of where the culture is headed; and any other important data points which impact your portagonist.

Brainstorm here:

Voice and Writing Style

Let's confront the enigmatic voice questions many writers ask: What is voice? Do I have it? If not, how do I get it? It's almost impossible to separate ideas of interiority from those of voice and writing style. If we're doing our jobs as writers, every time we inhabit a character point of view, we assume the character's voice and personality, especially in first and close-third POV. If we're using an intrusive narrator, we must also develop their particular brand of authorial voice.

Remember, readers want to care and connect. Access to character is the most direct route to this goal, especially when it offers layers of vulnerability, desire, objective, motivation, need, inner struggle, and growth. Voice can be a great craft tool that adds energy and dimension to these elements. But what *is* voice? Many literary agents and acquisitions editors simply say, "I know it when I see it." This answer is a copout, and a bit lazy, too. Of course, voice is incredibly subjective, so there's some truth to this statement. A more accurate brush-off would be, "Voice really depends on the writer, project, genre, and protagonist at hand. As long as the prose and dialogue are intentionally done, you're likely to be writing with voice. Whether it personally appeals to an individual gatekeeper is another question." But we're not here for the brush-off, so let's dig in.

The main components of voice are:

- Word Choice
  - Refers to each building block of your sentences—the individual words you're using.

- Syntax
    - This refers to the length and complexity of your sentences.
- Imagery
    - Relies heavily on the senses to describe setting and atmosphere, and the unspoken goal is often to immerse audiences in your story and offer a frisson of enjoyment.
- Emotion
    - The tone or intended reader reaction you're going for. Words have denotations—literal meanings—and connotations—implied meanings. Those connotations are usually emotional or even subconscious.
- Character
    - It all comes back to character. When you think of how old your character is, their cultural context and background, as well as their overall vibe, energy, mood, and position along their growth arc, you will start to tune your ear into what their voice might sound like.

Discovering and honing a protagonist's voice, regardless of point of view, is really the work of writing a novel from their perspective. What kinds of words and sentence styles do they use? How does their interiority differ from their dialogue? How might they describe the various stimuli in a scene? How could their reactions and interpretations be used to characterize them further?

Dry and Blurry Voice

One thing to watch out for is dry voice, as well as indistinct writing across different point of view characters. (Each character's style should be distinct in a multi-POV approach, and if they blur together, you'll have a problem.) Overly formal narration and dialogue often express simple ideas with needless verbosity, fussiness, or jargon. Yes, sometimes technical or archaic language is warranted, such as in a police procedural or historical story, respectively, but the overall cadence, sentence structure, and word choice shouldn't be challenging to parse, especially if you're writing contemporary fiction. To me, dry voice has no place in modern prose, not even for academic characters, those involved in STEM, legal, or medical fields, or supposed kids. Not because kids should be speaking in slang and dialect (please no!) or conveying simple ideas, but because they don't usually say "caused" and "vehicle." I cannot tell you how often writers who've created middle-aged-sounding "sixteen-year-olds" come back with, "But my character is supposed to be a prodigy, so they can speak like that." If a protagonist doesn't seem young to me, an older reader (*ahem* though I'm forever twenty-nine *ahem*), imagine how they'll come across to the actual target audience.

Revising Voice

So what should you do if you worry your voice isn't working? Sit down and play with it, sentence by sentence. Experiment. See what feels better. Too often, people simply read a writing reference book and bask in the theory, but they don't actually try what they're learning. If you recognize yourself in this description, get curious. Why not play around? What's stopping you? Take the pressure to "nail it" away and have some fun.

My other tip for developing your voice—and making sure it's working as you draft *and* revise—is to read the work aloud. Print the manuscript out and make marks in the margins for anything that sounds weird, or in places where you trip over your words. Yes, this is a huge pain. It will take a long time. You will probably get a sore throat. And, on top of everything else, your loved ones and neighbors might decide you've finally lost your remaining marbles. But this is a crucial exercise for every writer to do at least once, even if it's with a poem or short story. Voice is meant to be heard. I guarantee you'll learn something about yourself and your work by doing this experiment. (Actually doing it, not just filing the tip away.)

Odds are you'll spend your entire writing life developing your sense of voice, so there's no endpoint to this journey. Start actively honing your style today. Voice is one of those craft topics you'll be absolutely miserable about unless you relinquish control and enjoy where the ride takes you.

Dry Voice Revision Exercises

Take a shot at revising some of the following clunkers.

> They always had the ultimate respect for his sanctuary and announced their presence way in advance.

_____

_____

_____

> So many questions, but she had no time to ponder them.

_____

_____

_____

> The region's winter weather was moderate and would probably deliver survivable elements

_____

_____

_____

> But this time, the panic was real and consequential.

_____

_____

_____

In the awkwardness of the moment, she was at least grateful for her friend's reassuring demeanor.

_____

_____

_____

Trivial desires were brushed aside as I remembered there were questions to be answered.

_____

_____

_____

Voice and Style Text Analysis

Try unpacking the following examples of voice (and its elements).

Below, a small but significant characterizing detail is portrayed with imagery.

Voice Elements:

☐ Word Choice

☐ Syntax ☐ Emotion

☐ Imagery ☐ Character

Example 1:

The loss of his wife aged him terribly. No matter how hard he tried, he could never again seem to take a full breath in.

How is interiority used in this excerpt?

_____

_____

_____

How does this voice reflect character?

_____

_____

_____

Which elements of this passage work, catch attention, or create emotion?

_____

_____

_____

This character grieves a child she lost.

Example 2:

A memory crashes into her mind, a rip in the veil to another time. She stands in the park, a bundle of precious weight on her hip. Leaves shimmer in the sunlight. "Look!" But her words are more for herself than the child. To force herself to notice. Then suddenly, she's in the present again, her arms empty.

Voice Elements:

- [ ] Word Choice
- [ ] Syntax
- [ ] Imagery
- [ ] Emotion
- [ ] Character

How is interiority used in this excerpt?

_____

_____

_____

How does this voice reflect character?

_____

_____

_____

Which elements of this passage work, catch attention, or create emotion?

_____

_____

_____

> The next character is unexpectedly _cowed_ in a field.

Voice Elements:

- [ ] Word Choice
- [ ] Syntax
- [ ] Imagery
- [ ] Emotion
- [ ] Character

Example 3:

The cow sauntered up to me with a sultry gaze, its hot, alien breath tickling my skin. I wouldn't say it snuck up on me, but one minute the field was a barren wasteland and the next—_Bam!_ There it was, looming over me. Watching. Waiting.

How is interiority used in this excerpt?

_____

How is interiority used in this excerpt (cont.)?

_____

_____

How does this voice reflect character?

_____

_____

_____

Which elements of this passage work, catch attention, or create emotion?

_____

_____

_____

The following character kisses her crush at long last.

Example 4:

Tasting Allison for the first time is homesickness, a revelation, a memory. The sweetness of a summer afternoon, but aching like a bruised rib as she tries to catch her breath.

Voice Elements:

☐ Word Choice

☐ Syntax ☐ Emotion

☐ Imagery ☐ Character

How is interiority used in this excerpt?

_____

How is interiority used in this excerpt (cont.)?

_____

_____

How does this voice reflect character?

_____

_____

_____

Which elements of this passage work, catch attention, or create emotion?

_____

_____

_____

A workaholic character must pretend to be someone she's not for an assignment. She also has some issues displaying any kind of vulnerability. Can you see how these elements might play out in the following excerpt?

Voice Elements:

- ☐ Word Choice
- ☐ Syntax
- ☐ Imagery
- ☐ Emotion
- ☐ Character

Example 5:

Wearing a sundress with puffy sleeves, I felt like a stuffed Easter basket, leaking tinsel. The cool air fluttered up my skirt, reminding me how unprofessional this all was. Heads would roll when I got back to HQ. Lesson learned: Never leave home without a good pair of power slacks.

How is interiority used in this excerpt?

_____

_____

_____

How does this voice reflect character?

_____

_____

_____

Which elements of this passage work, catch attention, or create emotion?

_____

_____

_____

Our final example character is a woman with food issues who allows herself a binge.

Example 6:

I took the bubblegum-colored straw, wrapping my lips around it, gulping deep. Colors popped in my peripheral vision, a psychedelic dream of dragonfruit, cerulean blue, toasted coconut, Lisa Frank leopard-print waves, a sherbet sunset. The rum punch was a whole universe in and of itself, and I drained it all into my body without stopping to breathe.

Voice Elements:

☐ Word Choice

☐ Syntax

☐ Imagery

☐ Emotion

☐ Character

How is interiority used in this excerpt?

_____

_____

_____

How does this voice reflect character?

_____

_____

_____

Which elements of this passage work, catch attention, or create emotion?

_____

_____

_____

Voice and Style Checklist

01	Where possible, I've changed my verbs from "is" and "was" and reached for other actions that are more evocative. Strong verbs make for strong writing.	YES ☐	NO ☐
02	The nouns and other parts of speech I've used accurately contribute to the emotion and tone I'm aiming for.	YES ☐	NO ☐
03	I keep my adjectives and adverbs spare.	YES ☐	NO ☐

239

| 04 | My syntax (sentence length) is appropriate for the scene and mood. | YES ☐ | NO ☐ |

| 05 | I've avoided using overlong sentences in dialogue or to describe quick action. | YES ☐ | NO ☐ |

| 06 | I've used mimetic writing (a writing style that mimics the content) only when mechanics and style align with my scene's pacing. | YES ☐ | NO ☐ |

| 07 | I've cut out any instances of "purple prose" (a writing style which overuses description, adjectives, adverbs, imagery, and elaborate vocabulary). This tendency can actually make writing seem less confident than more masterful. | YES ☐ | NO ☐ |

| 08 | I trust that I'm getting my points across, so I avoid the temptation to repeat myself, explain, or pontificate on my theme. Though it's easier said than done, I trust myself and I trust my readers. | YES ☐ | NO ☐ |

Troubleshooting Interiority

This final set of exercises will help answer the most common interiority questions I've encountered since I first started working with aspiring writers and their manuscripts in 2009. Now, I have to level with you: Teaching writing is tough for one very specific reason—every writer is different, so is every story. Sure, there are patterns and categories and writing personality types which tend to have things in common, but I have to figure out how to package writing concepts for maximum applicability, while also considering what individual creators will find relevant to their unique projects.

With this in mind, I can't possibly pre-empt every question or cover every writing topic in a way which will be relevant to you. But I will try! And if you feel like you're doing brilliantly with interiority, you can skip this chapter—though I often find that writers really resonate with an idea after hearing it a few times, in different contexts, so the rehash might be worthwhile. Let the interiority questions roll!

What if I don't have any interiority?

If you've read this guide and are still wondering how to start filling your character's head with thoughts, feelings, reactions, expectations, and inner struggles, my advice is: go slow and answer the following easy questions.

What does my protagonist want? What gets them up in the morning?

What kind of person are they? What do they believe in?

If you're still stumped, try doing the same for yourself. You know more or less what's in your own head, right? Well, answer some of these questions in journal format. Do some stream of consciousness writing to get into the habit of paying attention to your thought patterns.

What if I'm not using enough interiority?

01   Review the major tentpole moments (see page 53) and identify them in your story. ☐

02   Read *Save the Cat Writes a Novel* by Jessica Brody to get your feet wet with plotting. ☐

03   Once you identify the primary plot points in your story, make sure you're supporting them with interiority. ☐

What if I'm using too much interiority?

01   Perk up your plot! Add stakes and introduce secondary characters and scenes. ☐

02   Look over your manuscript. If there's no white space on your pages because you're just in interiority or narration the entire time, that's a great signal to use dialogue and action to get your POV character out of their head. ☐

03   You should also probably trim some of your existing interiority, while you're at it, because self-restraint is always an option. Just get in there and kill those darlings. ☐

Can characters be too self-aware?

If your protagonist is already very self-aware and able to analyze all aspects of their identity, past context, and future goals, they might be *too good*. Or at the very least, unrealistic. Give your characters flaws and blind spots. Leave them some room to grow and change.

My protagonist's flaws:

What if people are finding it hard to care about my character?

		YES	NO
01	Is your character actively pursuing an objective?	☐	☐
02	Do they have strong motivations for doing so?	☐	☐
03	Are their backstory and character need relatable and compelling?	☐	☐
04	Revisit your stakes. Remember, stakes are our way of making meaning for characters *and* readers. Are they high enough on a story-wide scale and in individual moments?	☐	☐

If not, build some stakes into your story, scene by scene, by asking the questions on the opposite page.

What's the best-case scenario of this specific scene?

What's the worst-case scenario of this specific scene?

How does this specific event or internal turning point affect your character? (Remember: And? So?)

What if my character doesn't experience any meaningful growth or change?

There are indeed characters and stories that lack a growth arc. Read the following books and see if you care about the characters. You might find you develop empathy for them despite the fact that they're not redeemed or victorious.

- [ ] *The Guest* by Emma Cline

- [ ] *Ripe* by Sarah Rose Etter

- [ ] *Sing, Unburied, Sing* by Jesmyn Ward

What if I'm using too many dialogue or thought tags?

01   Stop it. No seriously. That's the answer. ☐

02   If you find this is your approach to dialogue and scene, have your POV character interpret other characters' true meaning and actions in interiority instead. ☐

03   Weave interiority into your narration or use italicized verbatim thoughts. Thought tags aren't needed in most cases, no matter your POV. ☐

What if I don't wanna do the work?

TOUGH STUFF

What if I'm writing a character outside of my own lived experience?

This is a serious contemporary craft and market question and I'm proud to address it. Diversity and owning one's own lived experience are huge topics of conversation in the current publishing landscape. A lot of well-meaning writers have found themselves in trouble over this issue. No matter what you personally think about it, or your stance on cancel culture, you need to be aware of this shift in the industry. I'm about to talk about diversity and inclusion as it pertains to publishing. While I'll use race-specific examples, this discussion relates to gender, sexuality, physical and mental differences, body size and function, neurodiversity, and any other axis along which humans can differ from one another.

There are some writers, literary agents, acquisitions editors, and readers who believe everyone must "stay in their own lane," which means only writing from the perspective of their lived experience. There are obvious reasons for this. For example, if you're a white person writing a Black protagonist, you're unlikely to deeply understand some of the broad facets and specific nuances of the Black experience. No matter how much research you do, no matter how you justify it.

There's also an argument that the white person writing a character of color —in a primarily white industry which platforms white voices—is potentially taking an opportunity away from a Black writer to portray a more accurate representation of the Black experience. The current position in publishing seems to say that main characters of color—or of a certain gender, sexuality, creed, etc.—should be written by creators who share that identity. There's tolerance for authors writing outside of their genders, but writers who cross race and disability lines, for example, are seen as much more problematic.

The "stay in your lane" approach does get ridiculous and restrictive for me, however, because stepping out of our own lived experience is the absolute cornerstone of both reading and writing. When we write a character, we step into someone else's shoes. Sure, our rendering is informed by our own lives, especially if we "write what we know." But writing is about taking on other perspectives. If you only wrote your experience, your books would be awfully homogenous.

So how does this square with perhaps the most hot-button issue in today's publishing culture? Well, I do think your protagonist should largely mirror your demographic profile, especially if you're writing and submitting for the first time. You might have opportunities to go farther afield with other characters once you develop a track record. When we get beyond the protagonist, there seems to be more breathing room. This means you should absolutely fill your story with secondary characters who reflect the diversity of our society, as long as you're able to do it intentionally, respectfully, and without stereotyping.

As I said at the beginning of this section, this advice might not be relevant to you, or it might be too general to be helpful. Given how prevalent this exact conversation is in the industry today, however, I'd be remiss if I didn't tackle this extremely polarizing topic in a guide on writing character.

Conclusion

One final question I've gotten from writers over the years:

Do I have to use interiority?

I mean, it'd be pretty funny if I said, "Nope, you sure don't." I obviously believe in this tool to the point of fanaticism. That aside, you don't have to do anything you don't want to do. I'm not your mom. (Joke's on me, my kids don't listen to me, either!) It's your manuscript, it's your writing, and it's your life.

However, remember seeing some of our example characters get walloped by epiphanies? Once you know, you can't really unknow. Sure, now that you've metabolized the amazing craft concept of interiority and the scales have fallen from your eyes, you can go back to writing the way you always did. You can suppress the blazing a-ha! moments you've had over the last 250 pages. You can absolutely ignore everything you've learned.

But would you want to?

Here's a simple call to action: Care deeply about your characters and make readers care, too! Sink below the surface of your protagonist with interiority, add layers, and ask lots of questions about your characters' experiences in big and small moments.

We're all works in progress, as are our, well, creative works in progress. By using interiority, you'll not only unlock additional insights into your protagonists, you might just live more deeply and richly, too.

The day you sit down to learn and understand interiority is the first day of the rest of your writing life. Storytelling is a journey in external and internal growth, and my most profound hope is that you enjoy the ride.

Kole

MARY KOLE

Resources for Writers

Since 2009, I've been creating educational materials for writers and designing courses, books, and services on writing and publishing topics. I regularly teach free webinars about query letters, character, interiority, plot, and first pages. Some webinars offer the opportunity for live feedback.

Please check out a current list of my upcoming workshops here:

goodstorycompany.com/workshops

I'm also available to Zoom into your critique group or design a presentation or workshop for a writing retreat or conference.

Work With Me

If you enjoyed this book, consider getting personalized one-on-one feedback from me. My specialty is deep developmental editing with a character focus. Alternatively, I am happy to step in as a discrete ghostwriter or offer direct ghost revision to execute any changes to you project. We can also work together in a small group writing workshop intensive setting.

Services

Developmental Editing Services:
marykole.com

Ghost Revision and Ghostwriting Services:
manuscriptstudio.com

Story Mastermind Small Group Writing Workshops:
storymastermind.com

Good Story Company

In 2019, I created Good Story Company as an umbrella brand so that my amazing team and I could collaborate in the service of writing and writers. GSC is where you'll find our most comprehensive library of resources and services.

Good Story Company:
goodstorycompany.com

Good Story Podcast:
goodstorypodcast.com

Good Story YouTube Channel:
youtube.com/goodstory

Writing Craft Workshop Membership:
goodstorycompany.com/membership/

Good Story Marketing:
goodstorycompany.com/marketing

Before You Go...

If you enjoyed this workbook, there are **three small things** you can do which would make a big difference to me and Good Story Company. Thank you so much for your time, kind attention, and consideration!

Subscribe to Our Newsletter

Our respectful, short, and non-spammy newsletter features all of our latest and greatest free resources, workshops, events, and critique opportunities. Go to the URL below to sign up:

bit.ly/hellogsc

Leave an Honest Review

Please also consider leaving a review for this title on your retailer of choice, as well as Goodreads. I love getting feedback of my own, and testimonials help greatly with my discoverability and marketing efforts.

Reach Out

Finally, I'd love to hear your experience and celebrate your accomplishments. If you run into some trouble in the writing and publishing worlds, don't be a stranger, either. Drop me a line:

mary@goodstorycompany.com

Also by Mary Kole

*Writing Irresistible Kidlit: The Ultimate Guide to Crafting Fiction
for Young Adult and Middle Grade Readers*

*Writing Irresistible Picture Books: Insider Insights Into Crafting
Compelling Modern Stories for Young Readers*

Writing Irresistible Picture Books Workbook

*Irresistible Query Letters: 40+ Real World Query Letters
with Literary Agent Feedback*

Irresistible Query Letters Workbook

*How to Write a Book Now: Craft Concepts, Mindset Shifts, and Encouragement
to Inspire Your Creative Writing*

Writing Interiority: Crafting Irresistible Characters

www.ingramcontent.com/pod-product-compliance
Lightning Source LLC
Chambersburg PA
CBHW052110020426
42335CB00021B/2699